CULTIVATING KNOWLEDGE AND WONDER

PERSPECTIVES FROM THE FRONTLINES OF TEACHING & LEADERSHIP

Presented by: Cicely Kelly Ward

Mac Media & Publishing

Cultivating Knowledge & Wonder

Cicely Kelly Ward

All rights reserved. No part of this publication may be reproduced, stored in a retrieval system or transmitted in any form or by any means, electronic, mechanical, photocopying, recording or otherwise without the prior permission of the publisher or in accordance with the provisions of the Copyright, Designs and Patents Act 1988 or under the terms of any license permitting limited copying issued by the Copyright Licensing Agency.

© 2024

Mac Media & Publishing

MacMediaPublishing.com

Print ISBN: 979-8-9919686-0-7

Printed in USA

"The true meaning of life is to plant trees, under whose shade you do not expect to sit."

- Nelson Henderson

This book is dedicated to the educators and leaders who stand on the frontlines every day, fighting for educational spaces that are inclusive, safe, equitable, joyful, and overflowing with curiosity and knowledge. May teaching and leading continually inspire us to create a world where everyone is empowered to learn, grow, and flourish.

TABLE OF CONTENTS

PART 1: NURTURE

CHAPTER 1
Nurturing in Instructional Coaching: Building Relationships Beyond the Transactional 9
Benjamin Glover

CHAPTER 2
Nurturing Educator Growth, One Relationship at a Time 19
Trelane Clark

CHAPTER 3
Nurturing Students with Intentional Teaching. . . 29
Chevalier Cross

CHAPTER 4
Seeds of Wisdom: Cultivating Growth in Teaching and Leadership 41
Dr. Valarie Harris

PART 2: INSPIRE

CHAPTER 5
Inspiring Scholars Through Physical Education . . 53
Letty Gonzales

CHAPTER 6
Beyond the Field: A Coach's Journey of Inspiring West Point Cadets and NFL Stars 63
Dr. Santario Stribling

CHAPTER 7
Building Bridges: Fostering Community and Collaboration Beyond Special Education. 73
LaKeeta Prunty

PART 3: TRANSFORM

CHAPTER 8
Leading with Love, Light, and Justice 87
Taisha Claytor Steele

CHAPTER 9
Building A Climate Of Trust 99
Machelle Brown

CHAPTER 10
Not Good, Better, or Best: Just Different 109
Deitra Colquitt

CICELY KELLY WARD

ACKNOWLEDGEMENTS

"If you want to go quickly, go alone. If you want to go far, go together." - African Proverb

This book would not be complete without the voices of the ten incredible educators and leaders who generously shared their stories and insights. Thank you for your wisdom, vulnerability, and commitment to building a better future for all learners.

Contributing Authors:

Benjamin Glover

Trelane Clark

Chevalier Cross

Dr. Valarie Harris

Letty Gonzales

Dr. Santario Stribling

LaKeeta Prunty

Taisha Claytor Steele

Machelle Brown

Deitra Colquitt

CULTIVATING KNOWLEDGE AND WONDER

VISIONARY AUTHOR

"Every educator has the potential to inspire and lead. This book is your invitation to step into that potential, embrace change, and discover new depths of your own knowledge and wisdom. Inside, you'll find a powerful combination of real-world stories and practical strategies ready for you to make an immediate impact."

- *Cicely Kelly Ward*

INTRODUCTION

A Mirror, a Treasure Chest, and a Compass: Tools for Transformative Teaching and Leadership

by: Cicely Kelly Ward

Three items stand out as must-have symbols for educators and leaders: a mirror, a treasure chest, and a compass. These tools represent both the successes and challenges of our journey. Much like these objects, *Cultivating Knowledge and Wonder: Perspectives from the Frontlines of Teaching and Leadership* is more than just a book—it's a guide, a resource, and a reflection of our potential. It serves as a mirror for self-examination, a treasure chest of collective wisdom, and a compass to help you navigate the shifts in education and leadership.

The Mirror: Reflecting on Our Practice

The mirror symbolizes self-reflection. It challenges us to look closely at our beliefs, behaviors, and impact on others. As educators and leaders, it's essential to examine our successes and areas for improvement, embracing both with honesty.

In this book, you'll find powerful reflections from individuals who have examined their own mirrors. Their stories of growth, struggle, and transformation invite us to reflect on our practices, encouraging the pursuit of continuous personal and professional development.

The Treasure Chest: Unlocking Collective Wisdom

The treasure chest holds the wealth of knowledge gained through experience. For educators and leaders, it's a collection of lessons, strategies, and insights that grow with time. The key is not only in accumulating this wisdom but in sharing and applying it to enhance our work.

Within these pages lies a treasure chest of ideas from diverse voices in education and leadership. Each chapter offers practical strategies, fresh perspectives, and valuable lessons that you can implement in your own practice, deepening your understanding and expanding your toolkit.

The Compass: Navigating with Purpose

The compass guides us, ensuring we stay aligned with our core values and mission, especially in the face of new challenges. It reminds us why we started this journey and helps us make decisions that reflect our deepest beliefs.

Inside, you'll discover how educators and leaders have relied on their compass to make tough choices, overcome obstacles, and stay true to their goals. Their experiences provide inspiration, helping you navigate your own path with clarity and intent.

The Road Ahead

As you read *Cultivating Knowledge and Wonder*, embrace these symbols—the mirror, the treasure chest, and the compass—as tools for growth, discovery, and direction. The stories and insights shared here are not just words on a page; they are invitations to reflect, learn, and reignite your passion for teaching and leading.

This book celebrates the power of collaboration, lifelong learning, and the belief that each of us holds the potential to make a meaningful impact. Open your mind and let it guide you toward cultivating both knowledge and wonder in your life and in the lives of those you serve.

Contributing Authors

Benjamin Glover is the esteemed owner of STEM Detective, LLC. As a multi-year Teacher of the Year award recipient, Glover has served as a science and math teacher, Teacher Development Specialist, and Instructional Coach. He is also the author of both *Do Nows in Science and SciMastery*. His commitment to revolutionizing math and science teaching through inquiry-based, student-centered methods has profoundly deepened classroom engagement and learning.

Trelane Clark is a lifelong educator, leader, speaker, presenter, and writer with nearly 30 years of experience serving public, private, urban, and suburban school students. She believes our children deserve an equitable education regardless of school or circumstances. Trelane's professional mission is to inspire educators to THRIVE-Teach from the Heart, model Resiliency, lead with Integrity, Value relationships, and ensure Equity for all.

Chevalier Cross is a dedicated and compassionate preschool teacher with over 26 years of experience in fostering the growth of young minds. She is committed to creating a safe, supportive, and engaging learning environment where children can build essential social, emotional, and cognitive skills. A firm believer in the power of play-based learning, Chevalier uses creativity and warmth to inspire curiosity and confidence in her students helping them develop a strong foundation.

Dr. Valarie Harris is an accomplished educator and leader with over forty years of experience in teaching and leadership. Dr. Harris has dedicated her career to empowering students and fostering a love for learning. Currently serving as the Director of Ministries at her church and CEO of Stepping Out with Purpose, she specializes in guiding women leaders and entrepreneurs. Her work emphasizes financial freedom, cultivating healthy lifestyles, and leaving a legacy.

Letty Gonzales has been an educator for over 35 years, dedicating her career to serving diverse, low-income school communities as a Technologist and Physical Education Teacher. After retiring in Spring 2022, Letty felt her purpose in education was not yet complete, so she returned six months later as an Assistant Counselor, a mentor for other PE coaches, and a presenter at TAHPERD conferences and professional development training sessions.

Contributing Authors

Dr. Santario Stribling is a retired public school administrator with over 23 years of experience in education, spanning elementary, middle, and high school levels. His career includes roles as a classroom teacher, athletic coach, and campus administrator. Additionally, Dr. Stribling is a retired United States Army Reserve officer, bringing over 32 years of military service to his background in leadership. Dr. Stribling holds degrees in Education Administration, Sports Administration, and a Doctorate in Education.

LaKeeta Prunty has been a dedicated advocate for families and students in her community for nearly two decades. With a dual degree in Psychology and Marketing Management and a Master's in Cross-Categorical Special Education, she brings a well-rounded and compassionate approach to education. LaKeeta is deeply passionate about cultivating strong relationships with students, nurturing their self-confidence. Her commitment to education is driven by her desire to empower the next generation.

Taisha Claytor Steele is a visionary leader dedicated to advancing justice and equity through compassionate leadership. Grounded in the belief that authentic leadership is about serving others, Taisha strives to create spaces where people feel seen, heard, and empowered to contribute their unique gifts. Leading with a deep sense of purpose, Taisha champions collaboration, diversity, and the power of collective action.

Machelle Brown is an educator and the author of *Authentically Me: Flaws & All – From Teacher to A.P.* and *Gabriel: The Silent Truth*. Brown's work, both as an author and mentor, inspires educators and students to lead with integrity, champion equity, and embrace the power of storytelling. Her efforts advocate for a more inclusive, student-centered education system, sparking essential conversations about leadership, diversity, and the need for unheard voices to be uplifted.

Deitra Colquitt is a passionate and dedicated elementary school principal, committed to showcasing the brilliance and potential within the students and community she proudly serves. As a product of the same district where she now leads, Deitra brings a deeply personal connection and a transformative vision, aiming to redefine the narrative for the children in her care. She strives to uplift and empower people of color, fostering an environment where they can thrive in their unique gifts and talents.

CICELY KELLY WARD

PART 1
NURTURE

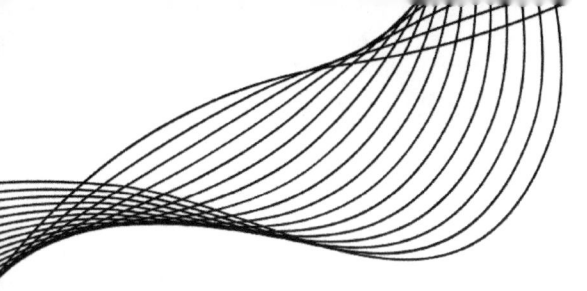

" Like a mirror reflecting the growth within, nurturing is the process of helping others see their own potential and guiding them toward their fullest development. At the heart of education lies this power to nurture—not just academic growth, but the emotional, social, and relational development that defines a successful learning environment.

– Cicely Kelly Ward

CULTIVATING KNOWLEDGE AND WONDER

BENJAMIN GLOVER

"Nurturing isn't just about what happens in the classroom or during a coaching session—it's about building a relationship based on genuine care."

- Benjamin Glover

Chapter 1

Nurturing in Instructional Coaching: Building Relationships Beyond the Transactional

by: Benjamin Glover

When I think about nurturing, I see it as a relationship transcending a simple transactional interaction. It's about the depth of care and commitment a leader brings to those they mentor, guiding them through challenges while focusing on their growth and potential. As an instructional coach, nurturing means seeing the good even in difficult or dire situations—finding those moments of progress and growth that others might overlook and building on them. For instance, when I walk into a first-year teacher's classroom and observe a lesson that may not go as planned, my role as a nurturing leader is to find the small successes and bright spots to build from there. There may be one interaction with a student that stands out or one well-structured part of the lesson. I take those few highlights and use them as a stepping stone to inspire the teacher, guiding them toward becoming the best version of themselves. Nurturing is like parenting—guiding, supporting, and reassuring them, knowing I've been through similar experiences and seen the benefits of consistency and growth over time.

This was particularly true when working with Karina, a fifth-grade science teacher I supported early in my career as a coach. Initially, she struggled to implement specific instructional strategies, and her confidence in the classroom was low. But nurturing her meant I didn't just tell her what she was doing wrong. Instead, I did the heavy lifting alongside her. I modeled lessons, helped plan her instruction, and even went as far as purchasing materials she needed for her classroom. Why did I do all of this? Because I wanted to build credibility. I wanted her to see that whatever I asked her to do, I could do and do well.

By showing her that my guidance wasn't just theoretical but was rooted in practical experience, she could focus on the two or three key areas that mattered most for her development rather than feeling overwhelmed by a long list of demands. Over time, as she built her capacity in those prioritized areas, I began to release more responsibility to her. The gradual release empowered her to take ownership of her growth, eventually leading to real, tangible success with her students. For example, as she refined her questioning techniques, I noticed her students becoming more engaged in class discussions, building on each other's ideas and developing critical thinking skills. They weren't just participating more; they were learning to think deeply and articulate their thoughts confidently. Another significant shift was in how students interacted with their progress. Over time, they became well-versed with their data—they knew exactly where they were excelling and where they needed support. They took charge of their learning, proactively seeking out resources for remediation or acceleration as needed. Instead of the usual 'I don't know' response when asked about their struggles, they began to say, 'I'm having trouble with this, but I'm using X, Y, and Z to improve.' It was amazing to see them identifying their challenges and articulating the steps they were taking to overcome them. Our relationship was built on trust and mutual respect, and even though I no longer work with her regularly, we still have a strong connection because of the nurturing relationship we developed.

When I think of modeling for Karina, it doesn't start in front of the students. The modeling begins in the planning process. I showed her how I would go through backward planning and think through the 5E components of the science instructional model: Engage, Explore, Explain, Elaborate, and Evaluate. I modeled these planning pieces distinctly because I wanted her to see the correlation between the diligence of planning and the quality of execution. When I stepped into the classroom to model the lesson, I wanted her to see how detailed planning translates into effective teaching.

During the actual model lesson, Karina is my student. I always plan what she should focus on, just like I plan for the students' actions. I give her specific areas to observe, particularly those high-yield areas that we've prioritized. After, we have a coaching conversation to reflect on what she noticed and to create actionable steps for both of us to follow. This keeps the process grounded and ensures continuous growth.

After the initial model lessons, we move to the co-teaching phase, where we plan the lesson together, but I still highlight the high-yield areas she's focusing on. During the co-teaching, I allow her to lead those sections of the lesson so I can observe how she implements them. I provide on-the-spot coaching during the lesson to help her adjust if necessary.

Following the co-teaching phase comes the "You-Do" phase. Karina takes full responsibility for the lesson in this phase, and I step back to observe. This is the phase where she takes full ownership of her classroom and her students' learning while I focus on assessing her progress and providing feedback after the lesson.

What's important to recognize here is that the gradual release has two sides: the teacher-coach side and the teacher-student side. On the teacher-coach side, Karina started to take on more responsibility with planning and lesson execution, strengthening her skills and building confidence. On the teacher-student side, she was stepping back into full ownership of her classroom, guiding her students independently, and becoming the leader in that space. This transition matters because it's where she starts to see herself as capable—both in planning and the classroom. As a coach, I recognize this shift is huge because it confirms to the teacher that they're ready to stand on their own. It's empowering; it's a moment when they realize they can handle it and are equipped to manage, adapt, and succeed without constant support. That's what builds their confidence and sets them up for sustained growth.

Consistency is critical after the gradual release process. Teachers need to maintain steady efforts, like marathon runners who pace themselves to ensure they reach the finish line. Building systems in the classroom is essential, but without consistent implementation, those systems won't take hold. Students must see consistent expectations and behaviors to fully buy into the classroom culture. Patience is also vital; students may not adjust immediately to higher expectations, but maintaining those expectations over time is essential for sustainable progress.

Student accountability significantly contributes to creating a positive and sustainable classroom culture. By establishing systems of rewards and consequences, we encourage students to take ownership of their learning and behavior. When most students buy into the system, others will follow, creating a culture where responsibility is shared. Empowering students to take ownership of their learning reduces the burden on the teacher and transforms the classroom dynamic.

It's also essential to celebrate successes. Recognizing both student and teacher progress fosters a positive environment. I leave notes for teachers like Karina, pointing out what they did well, and sometimes I'll offer small tokens of appreciation, like gift cards, to acknowledge their hard work. Building relationships beyond just coaching is essential for sustaining long-term growth.

Involving school leaders is another critical element. Since I'm not on campus daily, I make sure to keep school leaders informed about the progress of teachers like Karina. I share follow-up notes with the teacher and the leadership team, outlining the teacher's action steps and my own. This ensures that even when I'm not there, the school leadership can monitor the teacher's progress and provide additional support. It takes a team to help a teacher grow, and being aligned in our approach ensures that improvements are long-lasting.

A common misconception about nurturing is that it's solely about being gentle and reassuring. While those are important aspects, nurturing also involves accountability. If you're nurturing someone to their best, there will be times when you need to have difficult conversations. Accountability is an essential part of nurturing because it helps people grow. It's not just about saying everything will be okay. Sometimes, it's about saying this is the expectation, and here's why we need to meet it to serve your students better. Holding people accountable fosters self-motivation, metacognition, and resilience, so they learn to inspire themselves even when you're not there.

In my coaching practice, I hold teachers to high standards because I know what they're capable of achieving, but I balance that with patience, understanding that growth is a process and setbacks are part of that journey. I often remind teachers, especially new ones, that I've been where they are, and I know how tough it can be, yet I've also seen what's possible when you stay consistent, and that's what I want them to hold on to in difficult moments.

A crucial part of nurturing is leading by example. It builds credibility when teachers, especially those new to the field, see you are willing to be in the trenches with them. In my work with struggling teachers, I don't just tell them what they should be doing; I model it. I demonstrate what effective teaching looks like, how to build engaging lessons, and how to manage a classroom. This approach helps teachers see that the strategies I'm sharing aren't just from a book—they're practical, tested, and adaptable to unique situations.

When I think of my relationship with Karina, this was a significant part of why she was able to grow and succeed. By being present, leading by example, and doing the heavy lifting when she needed it most, I allowed her to focus on what mattered. Over time, as her capacity grew, she was able to take on more, and eventually, she became an empowered, confident teacher who understood not just what to do but why she was doing it. That's what nurturing looks like—it's about supporting someone until they can support themselves and continue to grow even when you are no longer by their side.

Effective coaching goes beyond what happens in the classroom or during a coaching conversation—it's about building a relationship based on genuine care. I often ask teachers how their weekend was or check in on their family members if I know they've been going through something difficult. When teachers know that you care about them as people, not just as professionals, they are more likely to trust you and to push themselves to meet the high expectations you set for them.

That's the essence of nurturing—it's about building trust, being present, and guiding teachers in their professional growth in a way that empowers them for the long haul. Teachers who feel nurtured are more likely to stay in the profession longer because they've built a sense of purpose, passion, and possibility. When I nurture a teacher, my goal is to help them improve their practice and instill the confidence to face future challenges with resilience and self-assurance.

To sum it up, nurturing is more than offering support—it's about being a guide, an accountability partner, and a source of inspiration. It's about building a relationship beyond the transactional, where teachers feel valued and empowered to be the best version of themselves. That's what I aim to achieve every day as an Instructional Coach, and it's what I believe is key to creating lasting change in education.

CULTIVATING KNOWLEDGE AND WONDER

PRACTICAL TIPS FOR EDUCATORS

1. Start with Small Successes

When working with struggling teachers or students, always look for small victories. Focusing on what's going well, even if it's a small part of a lesson or interaction, helps build confidence and sets a foundation for growth. This can apply in classrooms where students may be struggling—help them see their small wins to encourage progress.

2. Model and Lead by Example

Effective teaching and leadership are best demonstrated through action. Whether you're a coach or a classroom teacher, don't just tell—show. Model what effective teaching, planning, and classroom management look like. This gives teachers and students a clear, real-world example to follow.

3. Use Gradual Release

Whether you're working with teachers or students, use a gradual release model. Start by modeling or providing direct instruction, move to guided practice (co-teaching), and then transition to independent work where the teacher or student takes full ownership. This gradual handoff builds confidence and allows for growth over time.

4. Be Consistent and Patient

Implement consistent systems, whether classroom behavior management or teaching instructional strategies. Students and teachers alike need time to adjust to higher expectations. Trust the process, and give everyone time to grow and adapt. Consistency is vital to fostering long-term improvement.

5. Build Relationships Beyond the Transactional

Trust is the foundation of growth. Whether you're a coach or a teacher, take time to know your colleagues or students on a personal level. Show genuine care beyond their professional role, creating a stronger bond and motivating individuals to rise to high expectations.

ABOUT BENJAMIN GLOVER

Benjamin Glover, the esteemed owner and executive director of STEM Detective, LLC, an educational consultancy, stands out as a magna cum laude biochemistry graduate with over 15 years of experience in public education. His extensive scientific research background is complemented by a proven history of improving underperforming schools through a STEM-focused approach. A multi-year Teacher of the Year award recipient, Glover has served as a 5th and 8th-grade science and math teacher, Teacher Development Specialist, and Science & Math instructional coach. He is also the author of two books: *Do Nows in Science* and *SciMastery*. His commitment to revolutionizing math and science teaching through inquiry-based, student-centered methods has profoundly deepened classroom engagement and learning. Glover's dedication to transforming educational paradigms ensures a lasting impact on the future of STEM education.

CONNECT WITH BENJAMIN GLOVER

- @gloverbenjamin
- @gloverb_1 & @stemdetective
- StemDetective.com

CULTIVATING KNOWLEDGE AND WONDER

TRELANE CLARK

"Anything that is needed must have something or someone to tend to it in order to sustain it, keep it growing, or reproduce. Therefore, educators, I believe, have a responsibility to the children and families we serve to nurture each subsequent generation of educators."

- Trelane Clark

Chapter 2

Nurturing Educator Growth, One Relationship at a Time

by: Trelane Clark

She gave me the title of manager. I was only in the fourth grade. I had no idea what I thought I was managing, but she seemed to notice that giving me specific tasks that either supported her or helped other students added a certain spark to my place in the classroom. Although schoolwork was typically not difficult for me, I suffered from low self-concept and low self-esteem. I didn't know that she was not only providing me with opportunities to explore my gifts, talents, and strengths but also slowly planting the seeds of my interest in education. She challenged me, kept the rigor high, and held me accountable for my learning and whatever I was doing. She kept me engaged by highlighting the areas where I demonstrated significant skills and talking with me about them. She cared about my spiritual life just as much as my career trajectory. My fourth grade (and subsequently also eighth grade) teacher became my self-appointed godmother. By the time she retired from teaching after about 30 years in the classroom, I had been teaching for three years. Because of my godmother's constant support and unwavering faith, I carry pieces of her in me and through my practices as a teacher and a leader. I am blessed to still have her in my life, where she continues to support, celebrate, and counsel me in every area of my life.

Education is the industry that leads everyone into every other industry. No one gets anywhere without a teacher. Although our society does not always hold educators in the highest regard, I highly doubt anyone disagrees that we need teachers. We need leaders of teachers. Therefore, I believe educators have a responsibility to the children and families we serve to nurture each subsequent generation of educators.

I got my first "big break" into school leadership around 2009. This was on the heels of a traumatic chapter in my personal life. I was in graduate school to obtain my educational administration degree while teaching at a small, private Christian school. The school's owners and leaders purchased it the year before I arrived to prevent it from closing altogether. The school was struggling and needed structures and staffing that would keep the school afloat. I started teaching upper elementary and middle school students. Although the Head of School had a clear vision for Math and Science instruction, the same did not exist for English Language Arts and Social Studies. I asked the leaders if I could create a new leadership position for myself as Dean of Curriculum and Instruction to fill this gap. Naturally, they agreed because they knew it was a void at the school. This role allowed me to participate in the hiring and retention of teachers. I developed relationships with the teaching staff and got to know them as individuals and educators. They gave me greater insight into the types of support they needed and a sense of their professional aspirations. They also challenged me to customize professional learning by identifying resources, modeling lessons, and more. Whether early or mid-career teachers, I spent time with them planning units, discussing student achievement and data, and checking in with them on how they were caring for themselves. These one-on-one conversations made teachers feel more comfortable sharing their dreams and pain points with me, knowing I was always willing to learn alongside them. I took great pride in these conversations, knowing that it is always at the teacher's discretion whether to implement new learning based on evaluator feedback. The work of relational trust at the start fostered relationship building and a safe space for teacher growth to occur under my guidance.

In each subsequent school where I served as an assistant principal and ultimately as a principal, I continued working to build relational trust first and ensuring that teachers felt comfortable coming to me for support. In each school, I invite all teachers and staff I will supervise or with whom our work significantly intersects to have one-on-one conversations with me. These 15-20 minute meetings are optional, yet typically, over 80% of the staff members in a school scheduled time with me. It is never too late for anyone to make an appointment with me! I have questions in a Google Form and take notes on our conversation. I always inform them that my notes will not be shared with anyone else. I explain that once I have met with most or all of the stakeholders, I am able to go back to my notes to identify trends and patterns in what has been shared. Ultimately, this data provides me with a wealth of insight into where the school shines and areas where staff feels improvement is necessary. It becomes the basis for faculty meeting content, teaching and learning topics for professional development, school culture and climate ideas, and much more. Through these one-on-one conversations, they contribute to enhancing the whole school environment without realizing it! Even though I am prepared with a set of questions, I often allow the conversations to veer off organically so that the individuals begin to let down any guards and become more vulnerable, sometimes even sharing concerns that directly affect their work. At times, during these meetings, I am cautioned about potential pitfalls or where toxicity may be lurking in the background of the organization. All data is good data and, when used appropriately, can help support the overall effectiveness of the school environment.

I love what I can learn about individuals during these interactions. It reduces the number and frequency of those awkward greetings in the hallways that are void of connection. I try to get as many of these meetings done before the start of the school year because educators are often more relaxed, less pressed for time, and more candid. I begin these conversations by modeling what I am looking for from them. I start by sharing personal information about myself regarding my family, educational and professional experience, what I like to do outside of work, some strengths, and things that bring me joy. There is incredible power in these first few minutes to foster connection and familiarity. When some hear about how much I love to read, my passion for music, how I've embraced walking not only for physical health but also as a tool for mental clarity and generating creativity, and my guilty pleasures, like chocolate and peanut butter–a door opens for them with an instant opportunity to respond with, "Me too!" Then, I invite the educator to do the same by asking them to share what is important for me to know about them, first personally and then professionally. This distinction is significant because we sometimes get so caught up in our identities as educators that we forget to nurture the characteristics, hobbies, and pleasures that make us who we truly are. I also typically ask how they prefer to communicate and receive feedback. Knowing this vital piece of information can help to reduce instances of miscommunication and help critical feedback to be received effectively. Additionally, I often ask them to name their strengths. This gives them permission to brag about themselves and a powerful launching pad for me to highlight or invite them to share best practices with others!

Reflecting on my days as a classroom teacher, I was unfortunately hard-pressed to remember many positive experiences with the observation, feedback, and evaluation process. Although I was observed, I do not remember much feedback that changed my instruction. I do remember some of the critical, negative feedback that was delivered without clear next steps to support my teaching. So, I dug my heels into the areas of teaching that were the most interesting to me and searched to identify my strengths and work on my weak areas. Those teachers who are genuinely invested in the work will always stand out. I believe that I was one of them. I try to call out specific strengths when I see them. The teacher observation and feedback cycle, whether through informal or formal observations, should never be designed as a 'gotcha' where the goal is to catch a teacher doing 'wrong.' There must be learning opportunities for both the teacher and the observer. I work hard to be intentional about breaking down this perception. Most educators want feedback because they want to be their best for students. Whether it is a quick sidebar conversation at the moment, a sticky note on the educator's desk, or an email to a grade level team about the consistencies I observed from classroom to classroom, providing actionable feedback and then circling back to see what they tried differently is how we move instruction and therefore students, forward.

All I have ever endeavored to do as an educator is to provide an environment with structures and systems designed to give students what they need to be successful - equity. As a teacher, I had a modicum of control over this in the classroom. Yet, I always knew that as a leader, I would have the opportunity to influence this on a broader scale, impacting the lives of many more children than those who'd walk through my classroom doors. A few of the school leaders I worked under as a teacher saw my passion for leadership and supported my aspirations to move in that direction. Unfortunately, during the nine years I served as an assistant principal in different schools, I did not consistently receive the encouragement and nurturing I had hoped for. In one role, I was advised to take my "passion for curriculum and instruction, issues of equity, and teacher professional development and pursue careers that would allow me to engage in that work, as {they} believed I could be a valuable contributor. The message I received was that I was not an effective school leader. Thankfully, the universe saw me differently. The yearning from the depths of my soul, combined with the nurturing of mentors and school leaders in my networks, urged me to continue to pursue leadership positions, ultimately reaching my goal of becoming a school principal in 2020.

Reflections

In my leadership practice, I coach educators to see themselves as leaders inside and outside their classrooms. I encourage them to take risks and lead from wherever they are in the school. I have always told myself that, along my leadership journey, I always remember what it feels, looks, and sounds like to be a teacher. As a leader, part of my job is to usher in the next wave of educators as much as it is to see student achievement soar. School leaders must take the best of what we have learned and craft it into a style of leadership that is all our own – one that identifies educators' strengths, focuses on building relationships with them, and gets in the thick of learning alongside them. We strive to offer feedback that translates into a powerful, positive impact on our students' learning. When students see that school leaders support and care for their teachers, they will feel the same. We must tear down the barriers between school administrators and teachers that cause teachers to feel siloed and disconnected and rebuild pathways paved with trust, vulnerability, a shared vision for the achievement of our students, and heartfelt investment in teachers' professional and personal growth.

PRACTICAL TIPS FOR EDUCATORS

1. Share Your Story to Build Connection
Decide what story you will share from your personal journey to connect with your teachers and colleagues.

2. Encourage Meetings with Openness and Clarity
Invite, don't require, educators to have an introductory meeting with you regardless of their hire date. Be transparent about the purpose and content of the meeting. Keep the meetings short. Prepare your questions in advance and keep them the same for each educator.

3. Leverage Insights to Shape Your Goals
Use what you learn from those introductory meetings as data to inform your professional goals, learning, and priorities for the year. Again, be transparent and share overarching themes and topics that emerged from those meetings.

4. Engage in the Learning Process with Teachers
Get into the work *with* teachers. Don't just send them off to learn. Learn alongside them. Engage them in conversations about learning.

5. Acknowledge Strengths Before Giving Feedback
After having your one-on-one meetings, visit teachers' classes at least three times to note strengths and offer praise before offering any actionable, critical feedback to teachers.

ABOUT TRELANE CLARK

Ms. Trelane Clark is a lifelong educator, leader, speaker, presenter, and writer with nearly 30 years of experience serving students in public, private, urban, and suburban schools. She believes that all children deserve equitable education, regardless of school type or circumstance. Trelane intentionally seeks life's lessons, practices gratitude, pursues joy, and empowers others to do the same. Her professional mission is to inspire educators to THRIVE—Teach from the Heart, model Resiliency, lead with Integrity, Value relationships, and ensure Equity for all. She has served as the National President of Black Women Education Leaders, Inc. and as a Trustee at Concord Academy.

CONNECT WITH TRELANE CLARK

• • • • • • • • • • • • •

in @treclarkleads
@treclarkleads
X @treclarkleads
🌐 www.treclarkleads.com

CHEVALIER CROSS

"It's important to nurture and teach each child as a unique individual, recognizing their specific needs and strengths."

- Chevalier Cross

Chapter 3

Nurturing Students with Intentional Teaching

by: Chevalier Cross

As an early childhood educator, I often find myself pondering the different ways individuals process information. This led me to a powerful realization that I now share with parents and colleagues: everyone learns differently. This perspective is critical when you are intentional about each child as an individual. This way of teaching meets young children where they are and reaches challenging and achievable goals. Ignacio Estrada once said, 'If children can't learn the way we teach, maybe we should teach the way they learn.' This sentiment resonates deeply with me and guides my approach to education.

Connection comes before learning. When you form a genuine connection with a child, it not only makes learning more accessible and more fun for them, but it also lays the foundation for intentional teaching moments. When considering how intentional teaching may look for an early childhood educator, starting with a thoughtful lesson plan as a foundation is essential. This preparation includes creating a classroom environment that provides developmentally appropriate practice for the children. It is crucial as it allows the educator to observe each child engaging in play and learning to understand their natural interest. Finally, recording observations to evaluate the child based on developmentally appropriate milestones is essential. This thoughtful whole-child approach will help ensure each child receives the best support and guidance possible.

Understanding Intentional Teaching

When it comes to intentional teaching, the first step is to be genuinely present. This means quieting all outside noise and allowing yourself to focus entirely on the child. It's important to reflect on your role as a teacher and how your actions can truly nurture each child's development and learning journey. Being fully aware of the child and their interactions lets you connect with them personally, fostering an environment where they feel valued and understood. Your thoughts and actions should come from a place of compassion, ensuring each child feels supported in their unique path. All of this is purposeful in your teaching behavior and classroom management.

Case Study: Ethan and the Sensory Table

Ethan is a curious, tactile learner who loves exploring different textures and materials. He often spends time at the sensory table, experimenting with sand, water, and various sensory materials. I introduced science and math concepts through sensory play to support Ethan's learning. We explored measurement, volume, and cause-and-effect relationships through hands-on activities at the sensory table. By connecting these concepts to Ethan's interests, I was able to keep him engaged and motivated while supporting his cognitive and motor development.

As an early childhood educator, it's crucial to emphasize to parents the immense significance of the first few years of a child's life, while many may perceive children as simply playing. As early childhood educators, we recognize that they are actively learning through play. It's not just about constructing structures with blocks or Legos. It's about the intricate thought process driving their imagination and the skills they hone as they build these beautiful structures. It's truly invaluable.

Importance of Being Present

The importance of intentional teaching requires you to be present and fully engaged in the moment with the children. It involves taking the time to understand and appreciate their interest and activities. Connecting with them builds a foundation of trust and security, fostering a positive and nurturing relationship. This creates a perfect setting for children to be more receptive and open to learning from you. Recognizing and valuing each child as unique helps create a connection that provides them with a strong foundation to navigate the world, discover, and grow by closely observing children and tailoring our interactions to their specific needs. We can experience the wonder of seeing the world from their perspective.

Recognizing Individuality

Teaching with intention rather than going through the motions can have a profoundly positive impact on children. By focusing on building relationships, you lay the foundation for increased engagement and motivation, setting each child up for success. Your interactions with children become more purposeful, allowing you to be fully present, connect with them, and tailor learning to their needs. By paying attention to each child's unique characteristics and experience, you can create opportunities for growth and development. Intentional teaching is to build a strong foundation with each child. This starts with presenting yourself as friendly and approachable, letting the child know, "I'm here, I see you, and I hear you." Building a relationship involves finding out about each child, including but not limited to their favorite activities, family, strengths and weaknesses, friends, home life, and culture.

The Power of Play-Based Learning

In my classroom, we implement intentional teaching through play-based learning. For example, we recognize that a child who enjoys building with Legos engages in a complex activity involving fine motor skills, imagination, and executive decision-making. This child's play is an excellent learning opportunity. We can use their interest in building to teach other concepts, such as grammar or story dictation. Intentional teaching means finding what interests each child and using that interest to facilitate and extend learning. Play-based learning is not just about keeping children entertained; it's a powerful cognitive and social development tool. Children who play explore new ideas, test hypotheses, and develop problem-solving skills. For instance, when children build a structure with legos/blocks, they learn about balance, symmetry, and spatial relationships. They are also developing fine motor skills and eye-hand coordination. By integrating these play activities into our lesson, we can help children develop a wide range of skills in a natural and enjoyable way.

Case Study: Max and the Blocks

Max is a bright and energetic child who loves building with blocks. He often spends long periods constructing elaborate structures and enjoys explaining his designs to his classmates. By observing Max's play, I noticed he has a strong spatial awareness and an interest in engineering concepts. To support his learning, I created a series of activities that incorporated his love of building. We explored concepts like balance, symmetry, and measurement through block play, and I introduced vocabulary related to architecture and construction. By connecting these activities to Max's interests, I was able to keep him engaged and motivated while supporting his cognitive and language development.

Adaptability and patience are essential traits for early childhood educators. It's important to leave personal matters at the door and focus entirely on the children in your classroom. Young children are full of energy and curiosity, and they may not always follow the plan you have in mind. Being flexible and patient allows us to respond to their needs and interests in the moment, creating a more dynamic and responsive learning environment.

Professional Significance

Intentional teaching is beneficial not only for students but also for educators. The benefit lies in the effectiveness of learning; intentional teaching allows educators to connect with each child at their level, fostering a deeper understanding of their academic needs. This understanding is crucial to the curriculum's success and educators' teaching methods. It enables educators to directly address the educational needs of their students, creating a more cohesive and enjoyable learning environment for everyone involved.

Intentional teaching is significant for professional educators as it enhances development, promotes inclusivity, and improves learning outcomes. By embracing intentional teaching, we create a more equitable and effective educational experience for all students. This approach allows us to support children with diverse abilities and backgrounds, ensuring that every child has the opportunity to reach their full potential. I utilize a curriculum that supports children with diverse abilities and backgrounds in my classroom. One of the key components is phonological awareness, which not only celebrates each child's name but also uses their name as a tool to teach phonological awareness skills. These skills are crucial for young students as they form the foundation for literacy and reading. By incorporating students' names into various activities throughout the school day, I provide them with regular opportunities to practice and develop their phonological awareness in a familiar and comforting environment. This approach helps students recognize and manipulate the sound within words, laying the groundwork for their future reading skills.

Putting Intentional Teaching into Action

Implementing intentional teaching in the classroom involves a combination of careful planning, ongoing assessment, and responsive instruction. Here are some practical steps for integrating intentional teaching into your daily practice:

1. Identify Learning Goals and Objectives

Start by identifying clear learning goals and objectives for each child. This involves regular assessments to understand students' strengths, weaknesses, and interests. Use this information to set specific, measurable, and achievable goals tailored to each child's needs.

2. Create Personalized Learning Plans

Develop personalized learning plans that outline your strategies and activities to support each child's learning. These plans should be flexible and adaptable, allowing you to adjust based on the child's progress and changing needs. Include various activities that cater to different learning styles and preferences, ensuring that each child has opportunities to engage with the material in a way that works best for them.

3. Use a Variety of Teaching Methods

Incorporate a range of teaching methods to address different learning styles and preferences. This might include visual aids, hands-on activities, storytelling, music, and movement. Using various techniques, you can ensure that all students have opportunities to learn in a way that best suits their needs.

4. Foster a Play-Based Learning Environment

Create a play-based learning environment that encourages exploration and creativity. Provide various materials and resources that children can use to engage in open-ended play. Set up learning centers that focus on different areas of development, such as a block center for building, a dramatic play area for role-playing, and a sensory table for exploring textures and materials. Use these centers to support learning objectives and provide opportunities for children to practice new skills in a playful and engaging way.

5. Build Strong Relationships

Take the time to build strong relationships with each child. Get to know their interests, strengths, and challenges, and use this information to guide your teaching. Show genuine interest and enthusiasm for their ideas and achievements, and provide regular positive feedback to encourage their efforts. Building trust and understanding with your students will create a supportive and nurturing learning environment where children feel safe to take risks and explore new concepts.

6. Monitor Progress and Adjust Instruction

Regularly monitor each child's progress and adjust your instruction as needed. Use assessment tools like observations, checklists, and anecdotal records to track their development. Be responsive to their needs and adapt your teaching strategies and activities based on their progress and feedback. This ongoing assessment and adjustment process ensures your teaching remains targeted and effective.

Reflections

As educators, our role in implementing intentional teaching is vital in the early stages of a child's life. We can better support their growth and development by employing individualized assessments and understanding how each child receives information. This approach fosters a child's cognitive and social skills and builds a strong foundation for future learning experiences. Embracing intentional teaching allows us to impact each child's educational journey, helping them reach their full potential.

In nurturing students with intentional teaching, we acknowledge the uniqueness of each child's learning process. This personalized approach enriches their educational experience and instills a love for learning that will benefit them throughout their lives. We can create an engaging and effective learning environment by seeing each child as an individual, building strong relationships, and incorporating play into our lessons. As early childhood educators, our commitment to intentional teaching underscores the importance of personalized education in shaping well-rounded, capable individuals from a young age.

PRACTICAL TIPS FOR EDUCATORS

1. Allow yourself to focus entirely on the child and truly understand and appreciate their interests and activities by connecting with them.
2. Connect and be fully engaged in the moment with the children.
3. Build a foundation of trust and security.
4. Play-based learning allows children to explore the world meaningfully through hands-on experience.
5. Teach with intention.

ABOUT CHEVALIER CROSS

Chevalier "Tasha" Cross is a dedicated and compassionate preschool teacher with over 26 years of experience in fostering the growth of young minds. She is committed to creating a safe, supportive, and engaging learning environment where children can build essential social, emotional, and cognitive skills. A firm believer in the power of play-based learning, Chevalier uses creativity and warmth to inspire curiosity and confidence in her students, helping them develop a strong foundation for lifelong learning. Outside the classroom, she treasures time with her family, embracing joyful moments and creating lasting memories.

CONNECT WITH CHEVALIER CROSS

in TashaCross
CrossCreations

CHEVALIER CROSS

CULTIVATING KNOWLEDGE AND WONDER

DR. VALARIE HARRIS

"Empowerment unlocks the potential within ourselves and others. Through education and leadership, we plant seeds of knowledge and courage, creating a legacy of purpose and impact."

- Dr. Valarie Harris

Chapter 4

Seeds of Wisdom: Cultivating Growth in Teaching and Leadership

by: Dr. Valarie Harris

Every journey begins with a single step, and mine has been a vibrant mixture shaped by passion, dedication, and an unwavering commitment to education and leadership. As I look back on my path, I deeply appreciate the countless students and educators who have crossed my journey, each playing a vital role and leaving a lasting impression on my heart and mind. This chapter, *Seeds of Wisdom: Cultivating Growth in Teaching and Leadership*, is a tribute to their integral part in my journey and a source of inspiration for the next generation of educators.

For me, education wasn't merely a career—it was a calling. From the foundational moments of my teaching journey to the guiding strength of my spiritual values, each step has been a lesson in growth, perseverance, and purpose. My mission has always been clear: to empower future generations, ignite a passion for learning, and lead with a sense of purpose and heart.

The Power of Faith and Lifelong Learning in Education

My academic journey, a diverse mixture of experiences

including degrees from Norfolk State University (B.S.), VA Tech University (M.S.), and Liberty University (Worship Studies), has been both enriching and impressive. These experiences provided a solid foundation in educational theory, spiritual development, and practical teaching skills. I also earned technology certifications from the University of Virginia (UVA), enabling me to incorporate modern tools into my teaching practices. My commitment to lifelong learning culminated in a doctoral degree from Seraphim Ministries International Bible College, where I refined my expertise in educational leadership and holistic student development.

Faith has been a guiding force throughout my career, shaping my teaching philosophy. At Seraphim Ministries, I learned to weave values such as empathy, integrity, and compassion into my work, fostering a supportive and inclusive environment. This approach has driven academic success and nurtured students into well-rounded, purpose-driven individuals.

Cultivating Knowledge and Critical Thinking

One of the greatest joys of teaching is sparking a passion for learning in students. My approach has always focused on making education engaging and relevant, using storytelling to bring abstract concepts to life. Whether explaining goal setting, historical events, or scientific theories, storytelling helps bridge the gap between ideas and practice, fostering more profound understanding and retention. One memorable project involved students creating vision boards filled with personal and professional stories to share their workplace experiences. This exercise reinforced their knowledge and enhanced their communication skills, making learning both individual and impactful.

At the heart of my teaching philosophy is cultivating critical thinking and curiosity. I encourage students to question, explore, and seek knowledge beyond textbooks, creating an environment where curiosity thrives, and diverse perspectives are valued. Embracing these concepts will enhance the learning experience and prepare students to navigate a complex, interconnected world. By fostering inquiry, I empower students to become independent thinkers and lifelong learners, equipping them with the problem-solving and analytical skills essential for success in the 21st century.

Reflecting on my journey, I recall when technology emerged in classrooms. Initially, I was content using a typewriter, hesitant to embrace the unused computer in my classroom. A coworker with a tech background challenged me to explore new tools, and her guidance had a profound impact on my career. This shift opened the door to pursuing technology certifications, ultimately shaping my role as the lead technology teacher.

This experience taught me the importance of embracing change and lifelong learning. By continually expanding my skills, I have enhanced my teaching and empowered my students and colleagues to thrive in an ever-evolving world.

Evolving Education and Empowering Leaders

Education is an ever-evolving field, with new technologies and methodologies constantly reshaping how we teach and learn. Embracing these changes has been crucial to my effectiveness as an educator. Throughout my career, I have actively sought to integrate innovative tools and strategies into my teaching, enhancing student engagement and learning outcomes. Whether incorporating digital technologies into the classroom or experimenting with new pedagogical approaches, my goal has always been to create a dynamic learning environment that prepares students for a rapidly changing world.

This adaptability fosters academic growth and empowers students to develop the skills and confidence necessary to thrive in the future. By equipping them with the knowledge and tools to succeed, we prepare them for the demands of an increasingly complex and interconnected world.

Equally important in my journey has been the mentorship of future leaders. Offering guidance and support to students and colleagues alike has been one of the most rewarding aspects of my career. Helping others recognize their potential and strive for excellence encourages them to take on leadership roles within their communities and beyond. Empowering future leaders ensures that the values and knowledge imparted in the classroom continue to influence and inspire future generations.

Through mentorship, I have witnessed the powerful ripple effect of nurturing leadership qualities. The impact extends far beyond the classroom, as those I have mentored go on to inspire and lead others, creating a cycle of growth and empowerment that continues to thrive.

Expanding Beyond the Classroom

Leadership in education extends far beyond the classroom; it's about setting an example and inspiring others through action. Throughout my 40-year career, I've held various roles: Special Education teacher, student workplace coordinator, transition specialist, lead technology teacher, director of ministries, and web designer. These positions taught me adaptability, empathy, and resilience—key qualities for effective leadership.

As a student workplace coordinator, I witnessed students humble themselves in diverse community placements, from schools to grocery stores. They developed essential skills such as resume writing, interviewing, and portfolio creation.

Today, I see many of them thriving in their careers, reflecting the lasting impact of those early experiences. Leadership, to me, is not about a title; it's about making a difference.

My leadership journey continued after retirement as Director of Ministries at my church. This role revealed how our gifts create a ripple effect, impacting lives globally. Beyond the classroom, my passion for teaching extended to global experiences. In Ghana, I was privileged to conduct leadership workshops highlighting the universal power of education in empowering communities. Similarly, leading worship workshops in India and contributing to disaster relief efforts in Grenada broadened my perspective, emphasizing education's role in addressing global challenges and fostering cultural understanding.

It also led to the founding of my company, Stepping Out with Purpose, where I help women leaders and entrepreneurs build purpose-driven businesses. This work extends my influence, proving that education and leadership are lifelong pursuits. Through Stepping Out with Purpose, I empower others to realize their potential, helping them achieve financial freedom, healthier lifestyles, and lasting legacies. Encouragement and inspiration are powerful catalysts for transformation, unlocking hidden potential and driving personal growth. By nurturing a supportive environment, we create ripples of positive impact that extend far beyond the initial spark of motivation.

Lessons Learned

Cultural competence and inclusivity have been essential pillars in my journey as an educator. Understanding and respecting students' unique backgrounds and experiences is crucial for creating a supportive learning environment in today's diverse world. By fostering a culture where every student feels valued, we enhance their educational experience and equip them to thrive in a multicultural world. Recognizing the challenges students from diverse backgrounds face and providing them with the necessary resources enables them to engage meaningfully with others, promoting understanding and cooperation across cultural lines.

Reflecting on my career, it has provided invaluable lessons. From navigating the challenges of teaching to celebrating student successes, each experience has shaped my growth. A key lesson has been the value of persistence. Challenges are inevitable in education and life, but they offer opportunities to develop resilience, adaptability, and a deeper understanding of the process. Each hurdle has taught me the importance of perseverance in personal and professional growth.

The pandemic was a defining moment for me. Isolated from loved ones, I chose not to be complacent but focused on completing my doctoral dissertation. It required countless hours of reading, writing, and researching, but my determination carried me through. At 68, I proudly marched, proving that age is no barrier to achievement. Many slow down as they age, but we have much to give if we are moving and breathing. Now, at 71, I am more convinced than ever that my journey is far from over. This cultural awareness, resilience, and lifelong learning lessons have shaped who I am today and continue to guide my work and purpose.

The Seeds We Sow: The Legacy of Education and Leadership

In conclusion, understand that an educator's legacy is measured by the knowledge they impart, the lives they touch, and the changes they inspire. The seeds we sow in our students' hearts and minds grow into our world's future leaders, thinkers, and creators. As educators and leaders, we have the unique privilege and responsibility to plant these seeds with care, nurturing each one with patience, wisdom, and a deep commitment to their growth.

Though often small and seemingly inconsequential, these seeds hold the potential to transform lives and societies. They blossom into diverse expressions of human potential, from innovative solutions to complex problems to compassionate actions that heal and connect communities. The impact of these seeds extends far beyond the classroom, influencing generations to come.

As we continue to plant and nurture these seeds, we shape a future filled with possibility and progress. Every lesson, every word of encouragement, and every moment of guidance carries the weight of a future yet to unfold. The true power of education is not simply transferring information but cultivating the essence of what it means to be human: creativity, empathy, resilience, and vision.

 Furthermore, an educator's legacy is not limited to academic achievement alone; it extends into each student's personal growth and character development. We may never fully know the ripple effects of our efforts, but we can be confident that each act of teaching contributes to a larger tapestry of human advancement. We must remain committed to this mission, knowing that we are co-creating a better, more compassionate, and more innovative world with every seed we plant.

In essence, the work of an educator is an eternal investment in humanity. As we continue cultivating these seeds, we leave a lasting imprint on the world—a legacy that transcends time and place. This is the profound beauty of education: the chance to shape not just minds but lives and inspire future generations to carry the torch of learning, leadership, and service.

PRACTICAL TIPS FOR EDUCATORS

1. Lead by Example
Demonstrate the behaviors and attitudes you wish to see in others. Your actions set a powerful precedent, motivating others to emulate positive qualities such as perseverance, persistence, integrity, and enthusiasm.

2. Provide Constructive Feedback
Offer specific, constructive feedback that highlights strengths and areas for improvement. Frame feedback positively, focusing on opportunities for growth rather than shortcomings.

3. Set Clear Goals and Expectations
Help others set achievable goals and outline clear expectations. This provides a sense of direction and purpose, making it easier for individuals to take actionable steps toward their objectives.

4. Create an Inclusive Environment
Foster an environment where diverse perspectives are valued and everyone feels included. To build a supportive community, encourage open dialogue, active listening, and respect for differing viewpoints.

5. Celebrate Achievements
Acknowledge and celebrate successes, no matter how small. Recognizing accomplishments boosts morale and reinforces a positive feedback loop, encouraging continued effort and commitment.

ABOUT DR. VALARIE W. HARRIS

Dr. Valarie W. Harris is an accomplished educator and leader with over forty years of experience in teaching and leadership. Holding advanced degrees from Norfolk State University, VA Tech, Liberty University, and Seraphim Ministries International Bible College, Dr. Harris has dedicated her career to empowering students and fostering a love for learning. Currently serving as the Director of Ministries at her church and CEO of Stepping Out with Purpose, she specializes in guiding women leaders and entrepreneurs. Her work emphasizes financial freedom, cultivating healthy lifestyles, and leaving a legacy.

CONNECT WITH DR. VALARIE W. HARRIS

in @talktimeval
f valarie.harris.716
© @talktimeval
🌐 SteppingWithPurpose.com

PART 2
INSPIRE

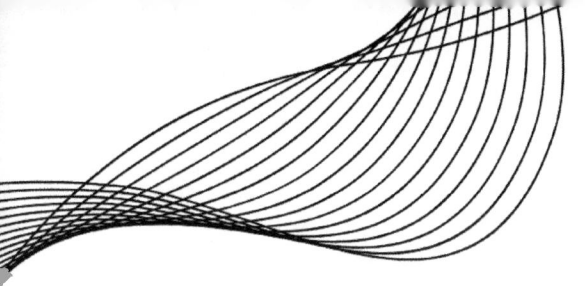

" Inspiration unlocks the treasure chest of potential within each individual, revealing hidden strengths and possibilities waiting to be discovered. It fuels change, igniting the spark that drives people to reach beyond their perceived limits and strive for excellence.

– Cicely Kelly Ward

CULTIVATING KNOWLEDGE AND WONDER

LETTY GONZALES

"Engaging at a young age can result in a rewarding and healthy lifestyle."

- Letty Gonzales

Chapter 5

Inspiring Scholars through Physical Education

by: Letty Gonzales

Do you remember the first educator that impacted your life?

I invite you to join me on a journey on how motivation, compassion, and belief from an educator can have a positive influence throughout a scholar's educational career and beyond. The first impression is very detrimental to how they will accept this encounter. We need to consider the location where we are providing physical education classes and how the information can be given so that everyone can understand and succeed throughout their journey.

The introduction to physical education can occur at a very young age. Active parents share those experiences with their family members, exposing their young scholars to an active lifestyle. In certain communities, some families do not engage in some of these kinds of practices. Regardless of the exposure, this is a crucial time for how movement and sports activities would impact a young scholar entering Pre-kindergarten or later. How a program is implemented could encourage a positive outcome, or a scholar might decide that sports or intense movement is not for them. Learning these aspects for the first time could produce an appreciation and enhance a curious mind to perform more movements. Based on how a scholar reacts could indicate if they would love setting goals for a healthier lifestyle or appreciate it to be able to make some changes that fit them later on in life.

Looking back on how I started my journey of becoming physically active in sports, I believe if I had not felt a positive welcome in that journey, I would not be in the position I am in today. With so many trials and tribulations in my young life, I would not have imagined myself pursuing such an amazing, influential career. My inspiration for my career goals happened in the 5th grade when I met Coach Middleton (Parrish) at my sisters' middle school cross-country meet. At the moment, I did not realize how she would impact the rest of my life. However, I felt a sense of encouragement and belonging just by conversing with her. Coach Middleton inspired me to discover my abilities as an athlete, but this was not an easy task as I had some difficult challenges to overcome while starting this journey.

In the 4th grade, unfortunately, I was in a terrible family car accident where my upper left leg was broken and where I lost my father. I was in the hospital for 6 months, then bedridden for another 4-6 months in a full-body cast. When the cast was finally removed, the doctor had stated to my mother that I would not be able to walk correctly even after completing therapy. As young children, we do not know how to process a response like this. I had already missed most of the 4th grade school year, going outside to play with neighbors, as I was already a very active child, and lying still was not something I found pleasing. I had difficulty understanding and would question why I was placed in this predicament.

Great coaches can encourage and let scholars know they believe in their abilities and potential to succeed, whether as athletes or individuals. Coach Middleton saw more potential in me and took me under her wing by guiding me throughout the summer of entering 5th grade. It began as a slow process as she would start me off with walking and power walking to strengthen my leg. I noticed that the stronger my leg was getting, the more I wanted to do and increase my strength ability. I began running, entering middle school. I felt so relaxed and free when running, giving me a sense of peacefulness. Running to me was a form of coping with everything happening in my life. We began strength training with minimal weightlifting as the coach monitored my ability. At this point, I was in full form to accomplish the task she was giving me, as I wanted to make her proud. She spent so much time helping me succeed in my goals to prove the doctors wrong about their diagnoses. I ran in cross-country and track meets; Coach Middleton encouraged me to play basketball, swimming, and volleyball in middle school. I placed 1st in many events, even setting cross-country and track records. I was so excited to take my medals to the doctor's office to show them they were wrong. My coach believed in me that I was determined to go further. When it was time to move on to High School, I was so pleased that Coach Middleton was transferring to the same high school I attended.

At this point, I knew she was my guardian sent to continue to watch over me as I was still facing the difficulties of losing my father and the challenges in my home. Coach pushed me even more to be the runner she knew I could be. I was training day and night for my long-distance events. I would run a total of 8 miles a day, and I would do strength training during PE class. She made sure our grades were up to par. Coach Middleton was by my side my whole running career and supported me with all my other sports, including various track and field events, volleyball, swimming, tennis, basketball, and football. She was like a mother, not letting me doubt my abilities. She would ensure we concentrated on school and our studies, not boys. I remember her questioning me about the tennis shoes I was training in and telling me to throw them away.

CULTIVATING KNOWLEDGE AND WONDER

Photo owned by Letty Gonzales.

The next day, she had a pair of Nike running shoes waiting for me by my locker. I also remember her taking me to the doctor for migraine headaches that she felt were being caused by all the running and my diet at the time. Coach Middleton always went above and beyond, even when she was going through her trials and tribulations. Coach Middleton's training led me to the state championship held in Austin, TX, where I placed 1st place in my long-distance events, the 3200-mile and 1500-mile run, resulting in setting state records that were held under my name many years later. Her influence and belief in me helped set my goal of becoming a Physical Education Teacher where I could help and impact different lives. My passion for being someone who could help change one's or many lives in a positive outcome will always be because my coach influenced me.

Upon beginning my teaching career, I was also able to coach the softball division at the neighborhood parks, along with having the opportunity to coach the softball team at my old high school, which allowed me to encourage many lives with positive influence. While coaching at the elementary level, I remember often speaking with scholars who needed that one person to listen and not judge them. I am so grateful they entrusted me with the opportunity to feel comfortable sharing. One day, shortly after I returned to campus part-time following my retirement, I sensed Coach Middleton's presence behind me as a yoga class began. I noticed a scholar hesitant to remove his shoes and join the others on the mats. Feeling compelled to understand his reluctance, I took him outside the classroom for a private conversation. He said he had no socks on, so I told him it was okay. Others were without socks, and he began to cry, so I told him not to worry. I started taking my shoes off, and he stopped crying and stared at me, not knowing what I was doing. I took my socks off, gave them to him, and said, "No one needed to know you could keep them." I put my shoes back on, and so did he, so no one would know when he walked into the room. When his class was leaving, he came up to me and just gave me a big hug. I knew at that moment I was in the right place at the right time. That same night, I called my children and asked them to gather any unwanted good socks as I gathered mine so I could take them to the school and place them in the closet for future scholars who might need some. There have been many moments where I felt blessed to be able to help scholars; this recent one will stay embedded in my heart along with others for many years to come.

A great coach's influence can leave a lasting mark early on or later in life. Witnessing the success of those you've mentored and encouraged is a blessing and a reward. I'm committed to continuing this journey of guiding and inspiring others for many years.

I've been fortunate to take on leadership roles and share my expertise with fellow educators throughout my career. I am honored to be a presenter for the *TAHPERD* conferences and the school district Professional Development trainings, during which we can share our knowledge with other colleagues. The *TAHPERD* Conference is the *Texas Association for Health, Physical Education, Recreation & Dance*. It offers coaches from across Texas the opportunity to gather and collaborate with presenters and vendors to enhance their skills and knowledge through other methods of teaching lessons and activities. I have been presenting in various sessions for the last 7+ years. I invite all colleagues, past, present, and future, to join and enjoy all the resources available to enhance our skills.

CULTIVATING KNOWLEDGE AND WONDER

For the last 6+ years, I have been a leader for the *Texas Outdoor Family Program with Texas Parks and Wildlife*, and I hope to continue leading and volunteering in this program in the future. This program helps engage families to come out and enjoy and explore the outdoors without worrying about the needed equipment as it is provided for them. This is a great way for coaches to influence outdoor activities for the whole family. Start this amazing adventure through the *Texas Outdoor Family Program* and become a volunteer.

In the summer of 2023, I completed my SEL*F and Yoga instructor training through *Breathe For Change*. As a yoga instructor, it allows me to present and teach mindfulness and poses to help others have a variety of forms of physical activity with low-impact movements and breathing techniques. Meditation allows us to recharge and reconnect to one's self. This great program is available for everyone.

Additional Resources

TAHPERD
bit.ly/3C4ZPPR

Texas Outdoor Family Program
bit.ly/TexasOutdoorFamily

Breathe For Change
BreatheForChange.com

PRACTICAL TIPS FOR EDUCATORS

1. Continue to learn and grow in your profession.
2. Connect with other colleagues in your field for needed guidance.
3. Keep an open mind on how to reach and reteach a variety of diverse scholars.
4. The simplest act of compassion can go a long way in someone's life.
5. A daily positive affirmation can help ground mindset and set a productive tone for the day.

CONNECT WITH LETTY GONZALES

@lettyygonzales
@lettyygonzales

ABOUT LETTY GONZALES

Letty Gonzales began her educational journey in 1992 as a Teacher Assistant. A year later, she accepted a position as a TA in Physical Education, where she served for two years. Letty then took on the role of Parent Liaison, and within the year, she was offered a position as Technologist for Kindergarten through 5th grade, a role she held for 10 years. During this time, she also began her studies at HCC, aspiring to become a Coach.

After two years at another school, her former Principal offered her a technology role on the condition that she complete her degree. Despite the challenges of being a single mother of five, Letty graduated with her Bachelor of Science and obtained her Physical Education Teacher certification from Texas Southern University in 2010. She spent two more years in technology before transitioning to a Physical Education role, where she worked with Pre-K through 5th-grade students for nine years.

Retiring in the spring of 2022, Letty quickly discovered her passion for education was as strong as ever. Just six months later, she returned as an Assistant Counselor/Lecturer, while also mentoring PE coaches and presenting at TAHPERD Conferences and Professional Development Trainings. In 2023, she was nominated and voted Chairperson for Recreational and Outdoor Adventure at TAHPERD's 100th Annual Conference, a role she will hold for three years. In the summer of 2024, Letty became a certified SEL*F/Yoga Instructor, continuing to advance her impact.

Letty is a proud mother to five wonderful adult children and their spouses—Misty-Marie Gonzales, Jorge Herrera, Arielle-Yvonne Gonzales & Ramiro Cruz, Desiree-Alexus & Juan E. Garcia Jr., and Robert III (BJ) & Ruth Gonzales—and a loving grandmother to Audrey Bella Cruz, fondly known as "Chunky Monkey."

LETTY GONZALES

CULTIVATING KNOWLEDGE AND WONDER

DR. SANTARIO STRIBLING

"True growth comes from personalized support, understanding unique needs, and fostering an environment where inspiration can thrive—whether sparked by others or found within oneself."

- *Dr. Santario Stribling*

Chapter 6

Beyond the Field: A Coach's Journey of Inspiring West Point Cadets and NFL Stars

by: Dr. Santario Stribling

In Senator Edward M. Kennedy's eulogy of his brother, Robert F. Kennedy, at St. Patrick's Cathedral, New York City, on June 8, 1968, he stated:

> *"Some men see things as they are and say why. I dream things that never were and say why not."*

I believe the ability to inspire is truly a gift. I also think that inspiration is the genesis of an individual's success. However, my experiences as an educator taught me that you must occasionally nurture students during the development phase. This development phase enables many students to use nurturing as a "bridge" to inspiration.

My Educational Journey

My parents gave me all the support I needed to be a successful student. However, that support didn't resonate enough to inspire me to excel in school. In high school, my academic life was pedestrian at best because I was not inspired to be a good student. Now, I have earned a terminal degree in my profession. What changed? Let's examine the transformation.

I am a retired school administrator and a US Army Reserve officer with the rank of Lieutenant Colonel. I have earned bachelor's, master's, and doctorate degrees. My father served in Vietnam and eventually retired from the Mississippi Army National Guard, so when my father suggested I join the military during my senior year of high school, I trusted my father's suggestion and joined the Army. This decision would impact my entire life. I was fortunate to have my father provide guidance throughout my lifetime; he was my first mentor. The success that I have had throughout my life has my father's fingerprints all over it, even though he has been gone for over 20 years.

My father couldn't offer me specific career guidance that extended past my hometown of Philadelphia, Mississippi. Fortunately, as I matured, I was mentored by professionals who guided me into realizing the opportunities an education could provide. This mentorship provided insight and perspective to broaden my vision, helped me challenge assumptions, and uncovered new opportunities. Also, this mentoring helped me develop self-confidence and awareness, offered me encouragement and motivation, and provided direction to the requirements of such careers.

I was mentored by professionals of all backgrounds. However, the defining cornerstone of my development was when I was mentored by African American males who looked like me, came from similar circumstances as me, spoke the same as me, and could understand the unique challenges that African American males in this competitive society may face. Because of this, I listened closely and observed them more intensely as they modeled career ambitions. When I saw someone with the same circumstance as me achieve success, subliminally, I thought to myself, "It can be done."

This led to my enthusiasm for becoming a better student, subsequently moving me to become a better professional educator and Army officer. Revisiting my earlier question of, "What changed?" What changed was this mentorship nurtured and inspired me.

My Inspiration

I have been inspired, and I hope to inspire others. My inspiration occurred when I was a teacher at Pflugerville Independent School District. We had a guest speaker for a staff professional development day. Her presentation focused on multicultural education and the diverse student population of our underserved communities. Her content and delivery were so impressive that I wanted to be part of the solution. In addition, she held a doctorate, which inspired me to further my education by pursuing my master's degree and eventually earning it. This guest speaker, whom I've never met, stimulated something inside of me to become a better student, educator, and professional.

I've coached numerous students who are thriving as successful adults. My goal has always been to motivate each student, empowering them to reach their full potential. I've taught three students who went on to the NFL and countless others who have excelled in diverse professional fields. I'm proud of every one of them; however, two students stand out when I think about nurturing and inspiration. The first is Ricky (a pseudonym). Ricky's story taught me that sometimes before you can inspire a student, you must first nurture them.

The Nurturing of Ricky

Ricky, a 7th-grade student, excelled on the football field. Unfortunately, his immaturity led to minor troubles, warranting my attention. Despite this, he was always respectful during our interactions, suggesting a potential connection. On the football field, his leadership qualities pointed toward quarterback potential. Yet, his immaturity off the field prevented him from gaining the head coach's endorsement to play quarterback. Nonetheless, I believed I could guide him to be a better student-athlete regardless of position.

Daily interaction on the field and classroom follow-ups revealed Ricky's misplaced priorities. His leadership potential was undeniable. However, the head coach remained unconvinced due to Ricky's behavior and grades. I believed assigning him the quarterback role would give him team leadership responsibilities and encourage improvement off the field.

Ricky eventually played running back, and he did well. He remained eligible for the whole football season, but when football season transitioned to basketball season, Ricky failed to keep his academic eligibility to play according to league guidelines. The shame of the situation was Ricky was the best player in our basketball tryouts. Consequently, our head coach wouldn't allow Ricky to be on the basketball team due to his academic situation, even though there would be a review every three weeks to determine their eligibility. Even the head coach seemed satisfied, inferring "told you so" when he learned about Ricky's academic ineligibility status. I felt it was my responsibility to counter that perceived pessimistic perspective from the head coach by nurturing Ricky to be a better student-athlete.

Ricky's mother and stepfather were always available for the coaches. Still, I felt that his stepfather's priority was keeping Ricky eligible for athletics, not the long-term goal of becoming a better student-athlete. I wanted Ricky to overcome his shortcomings and inspire him to seize his academic future. I continued to mentor Ricky during the remainder of my time at the school. I constantly reminded him of the possibilities available. I would share my personal experiences that led to my maturation with him and how I overcame them and became a better student. I expressed that his success would be within his reach if he modified his priorities.

In 2012, I accepted a new opportunity as an assistant principal. Drawing from my inspiration from the guest speaker I cited earlier in this paper, I had prepared myself academically to be qualified to serve as a Texas public school campus administrator; I wanted to expand my educational footprint to reach more students. As I settled into my new position, through social media, I would check on former student-athletes that I coached to see their progress. As I looked, I could not find any information on Ricky. The one thing I did find out was that he had left the school district the same year that I left. At this time, he would have been going to the 9th grade.

In April 2016, I received a message from Ricky through my Instagram account. I realized this was his senior year in high school, and May would be his graduation month. I was a little nervous to hear about what he was recently doing because I remember his immaturity as a middle school student; in addition, no one knew where he was. I have seen how fragile these young men's lives are and how one poor decision can disrupt a promising future. I hoped this wasn't the case with Ricky.

I was pleasantly surprised to learn that Ricky was about to graduate high school and earned a football appointment at the United States Military Academy. In addition, he had earned his football appointment to West Point, where he played quarterback, the position that I advocated for him in middle school. I felt a certain measure of redemption because of that. A West Point appointment is no small event, which is truly something to be proud of. The typical potential West Point Cadet football player must have excellent grades, get nominated by an elected official for consideration, and excel on the field, displaying leadership qualities that could eventually translate into a commissioned officer in the US Army. Many students apply every year, but only a fraction are accepted.

When Ricky and I communicated, he thanked me for nurturing him and asked me to help him become a commissioned officer in the United States Army. When I heard all of this, it made me proud. Not only was I able to be his coach, but I could also provide real-world guidance for him in his career.

The Inspiration of Eric

Eric (also a pseudonym) played football at the same school as Ricky a couple of years prior. Eric was small in stature, but he wanted to play. He was a "B-Team" player who rarely played even on the B-team level. Fortunately for him, UIL grades came due as the season progressed, and we lost several players to UIL eligibility requirements. Eric was a good student, and he remained eligible to play. By default, Eric advanced to starting fullback. He played most of the time in the following game but didn't carry the ball. The next day, he asked me why he didn't carry the football; I explained his "shortcomings" to him, and he listened and did not complain.

I coached Eric again the following year, but by the middle of the school year, I left the district and moved to Houston to another school district. As I mentioned previously, I would follow the student-athletes I once coached. In 2007, his team made it to the Texas State Football Championship, and I attended it. I saw Eric, who had grown into an athlete and was very aggressive on the football field. He was a starter for his varsity team. I even heard he was getting recruited by Division One programs. I didn't have the opportunity to talk to him at the game, but I was still proud of him.

Eventually, I returned to the school where I had previously coached Eric. By this time, Eric was playing Division I football. Eric and several other players came by the school to talk with our students. When I spoke to Eric, I thought his reaction would be, "Look at me now, Coach." But he didn't. He thanked me for challenging him. I asked him, "What made him continue to play at the high school level after leaving middle school?" He said that he listened to my constructive criticism and got better. He said he knew he could do it. Also, it didn't hurt that he had grown to 6 foot 2 inches and was very athletic. He went on to play in the NFL.

Years later, as his NFL days began to end, he announced his retirement from football. I texted him that I was proud of him and that he'd be fine with whatever he decided to do. He said, "Yes sir, thanks. You gave me a speech one time that I never forgot, and when times got tough, I remembered your words, no lie." I replied to him, "I'm just happy that I was a part of your education. Makes me feel good." I was like, wow! When he was in the NFL, he remembered my words from when he was a middle school football player. I was astonished, but it reminded me why I chose the education field in the first place.

Reflections

Reflecting on my journey as a student and professional educator, I recognize that nurturing and inspiration have been constant throughout my progression. Nurturing and inspiration are key to personal growth, with nurturing laying the groundwork for inspiration to take root. It's about offering personalized support, recognizing each person's unique needs, and creating the right environment for them to thrive. Though often sparked by others, inspiration can also be personal and transcend beyond physical presence.

PRACTICAL TIPS FOR EDUCATORS

1. Patience
Practice and exercise patience. It's essential to hold students accountable, yet remember, we are adults with lived experience and have seen our actions' consequences (good or bad). Many times, students have yet to develop insight into the consequences of their actions or lack thereof.

2. Persistence
Remain Persistent. Persistence and developing GRIT (Growth, Resilience, Instinct & Tenacity) have been the foundation of my journey as a student and educator. I have achieved many of my goals because of my persistence. This persistence should also be extended to students when mentoring them.

3. Optimism
Remaining optimistic in trying times is another cornerstone of my education journey. Optimism has always been the foundation of my motivation to support students. This is an essential component of a growth mindset, as the educator shall maintain a positive attitude despite possible setbacks.

4. Empathy
Empathize with your students as they go through their educational journey. We do not know everything that goes on in each student's life. Students' missteps can result from being undisciplined, yet their missteps can be a reaction to something in their environment that we may or may not be aware of. Regardless, educators should provide support through empathy for their student's educational journey as they guide them.

5. Mindset
Educators should embrace a growth mindset. This is the belief that one's skill and qualities can be cultivated through effort and perseverance. In a growth mindset, learning and growing is the primary goal. Educators and students should accept challenges and persist despite early setbacks.

ABOUT DR. SANTARIO STRIBLING

Dr. Santario Stribling is a retired public school administrator with over 23 years of experience in education, spanning elementary, middle, and high school levels. His career includes roles as a classroom teacher, athletic coach, and campus administrator. Additionally, Dr. Stribling is a retired United States Army Reserve officer, bringing over 32 years of military service to his background in leadership.

Dr. Stribling holds a Bachelor of Science degree in Education from Mississippi State University, along with two Master's degrees—one in Education Administration from Tarleton State University and another in Sports Administration from the University of Houston. He earned his Doctorate in Education from the University of Houston.

CONNECT WITH DR. SANTARIO STRIBLING

- SandyStriblingEd.D
- @santario5
- @santario5

CULTIVATING KNOWLEDGE AND WONDER

LAKEETA Q. PRUNTY

"Education is more than a lifestyle; it is a calling to partner with parents, students, and the community to create a path of social well-being and academic success while providing support, love, patience, and guidance."

-LaKeeta Q. Prunty

Chapter 7

Building Bridges: Fostering Community and Collaboration Beyond Special Education

by: LaKeeta Q. Prunty

Why Educate?

Why did I choose to become an educator, a Special Education Teacher? How can I reach students? How can I collaborate with my colleagues? Build a sense of community? If we are working towards a common goal, why is everyone against each other? Are educators supposed to be kind? These are some of the questions I have dealt with over the years in teaching in PK through the 12th-grade educational system. I chose to be an educator because I am passionate about learning and want to share my excitement with students and colleagues. My true passion is teaching Special Education students.

Unique Challenges and Isolation in Special Education

Special Education educators face the challenge of fostering confidence in students who often hear they can't grasp the same concepts as their peers. We also bear the responsibility of advocating for and educating our colleagues about the needs of these students. In my experience, many general education teachers fail to view special education students as their own despite having them in their classrooms for an entire year. This lack of connection can harm how students perceive the school and its staff. Building strong relationships with students is vital; academic success is more achievable when these connections exist.

Unfortunately, there is often a divide between students who display challenging behaviors and those who remain quiet or shy, exacerbating academic gaps. All students must feel that someone cares about them regardless of their behavior.

Being a special educator, particularly one of color, can be both physically and mentally exhausting. Representation in the EC-12 education system is minimal, and I have often found myself as the sole special educator of color, needing more support for my ideas and experiences. The isolation in special education is compounded by insufficient training and resources. Unlike general education teachers, who usually receive collaborative planning time, special education teachers frequently lack such opportunities, leaving us to take work home or stay late after dealing with challenging behaviors throughout the day. This situation contributes to burnout, leading many special education teachers to leave our profession. Often, we go unnoticed, a forgotten piece of the educational puzzle.

The Power of Teamwork & Partnerships

My experience in education has been a mix of positive and negative moments. For three of my years as an educator, I have found other educators who have a genuine sense of teamwork and share my belief that all students can learn and are willing to go the extra mile to ensure their academic and social-emotional success. During my fourth year of teaching, I truly felt I belonged. My team included special and general education teachers, and we held ourselves and our students accountable for their learning while fostering a supportive environment.

We collaborated closely on curriculum and student progress, and our effectiveness caught the attention of our principal, who wanted other teams to emulate our approach. We proudly called ourselves the "A Team," recognizing that our success depended on unity. We understood the importance of presenting a united front to our students; for instance, if a student asked one of us for permission to do an activity, such as going to another teacher's classroom while in another teacher's classroom, we would redirect them to the appropriate teacher. We would also ask that teacher so we could stay unified and support each other.

Our communication was open and honest, even when confronting difficult emotions. Whether joyful or challenging, every discussion was rooted in care and respect, strengthening our bond. I miss that sense of wholeness and connection. Effective communication among team members is essential for addressing our students' emotional and academic needs. The dynamics of a team significantly influence student behavior, as we serve as role models for them.

One of the key elements that made our team exceptional was our commitment to involving parents in the learning process. This collaboration boosted our students' academic success and reduced inappropriate behaviors. We recognized that parents are vital partners in education, and we knew we couldn't achieve our goals without their support.

We kept parents informed about their child's progress to emphasize their importance. We made it a point to call them with updates on any improvements—academic or behavioral—regardless of how small. Sharing these successes demonstrates our investment in their child's education and reinforces the idea that we all recognize their child's potential. Parents are often aware of their children's struggles but appreciate when someone acknowledges their strengths.

As a result of our united efforts, our special education students could master many concepts alongside their general education peers, even achieving high scores on assessments like the State of Texas Assessments of Academic Readiness (STAAR).

When Teamwork Fails

Unfortunately, our team was divided the following year, and the atmosphere changed dramatically. We were paired with individuals who didn't listen to all team members, lacked enthusiasm for every student, and didn't offer support to one another. Instead of fostering a positive environment, they focused on the negatives, often complaining without proposing solutions.

Two of us were reassigned to another team, while three stayed at the same grade level but with different colleagues. The principal believed spreading us out would be beneficial, but it was a mistake. The new team struggled with communication and made members feel isolated. For instance, when one team member fell ill, rather than offering help, they chose to gossip about her. This behavior was a stark contrast to the supportive environment I was used to, and it deeply upset me. I surprised myself by speaking up on her behalf, as I felt it was unjust.

This negativity affected my motivation and strained the relationships I tried to build. I entered the year with a positive outlook but gradually felt disheartened. I remained focused on my purpose—the students—but I found it challenging to thrive in such a toxic atmosphere. Being surrounded by colleagues who didn't appear to believe in our students was disheartening.

I held onto hope that discussions about team dynamics would lead to positive changes, but they didn't bring us closer or improve treatment among team members. I vividly remember one colleague asking, "Can you at least act like you like them?" referring to the students, which left me questioning why someone would choose to become a teacher in the first place.

Remembering "My Why" & Building Relationships

I hope the challenges we face as educators aren't dismissed simply because of the summer months. Even in June and July, we engage in training and skill development to enhance our ability to provide effective academic strategies for our students. By the end of the school year, the thought of summer can be enticing, especially considering our many roles—acting as parents, counselors, and sources of stability for our students amidst their struggles outside of school.

We shouldn't confine teaching to a 7:15 am to 3:15 pm schedule as it is a continuous commitment, especially when we've built meaningful relationships with our students. They become like family to us. At the start of each year, I emphasize to my students that we are a family, even if they jokingly point out that we aren't related. I remind them that

I've chosen to have them in my classroom and that they are my best students.

Special education students must hear positive affirmations about their abilities, as they often receive negative feedback about what they can't do. This approach helps build their confidence. When students feel seen and understood—despite their challenges and behavioral issues—they are more likely to exhibit positive behaviors. I strive to encourage my students to reach their potential beyond the classroom, understanding that sometimes it takes someone to believe in them.

My role is to plant seeds of belief and nurture them. While I may not always witness their total growth, I continue to support them, instilling the confidence they need to believe in themselves.

Supporting parents is vital to special education, as they play an essential role in their children's lives and our support team. Parents must feel someone genuinely cares about their children, especially during behavioral challenges. Many parents feel isolated, as family and friends may distance themselves due to their child's behavior, leaving them reluctant to share their struggles.

Advocating for Parents, Positivity & Collaboration

I aim to build trust with these parents, ensuring they know I'm not here to judge but to help them address and reduce challenging behaviors. I want them to feel confident that I care about their child, which opens the door to a deeper connection. Often, parents need a compassionate ear—someone who will listen without belittling or blaming them for their circumstances.

As educators, we may not fully understand the complexities of their experiences, but it is our responsibility to offer love and grace. We can encourage growth for the students and their families by fostering this supportive environment.

After all the training focused on nurturing and empowering our students, one might expect educators to actively implement these principles in their daily practice. As teachers, do we strive to find the good in our students, or do we take on the role of judge and jury? When students have faced challenges and setbacks, do we lift them or inadvertently push them down further?

For instance, when a student acts out—like hitting another student—they often face consequences. However, it's crucial not to assume the behavior solely reflects their character. Students are attuned to our energy; they can sense when we harbor negative feelings towards specific individuals. Yes, some students resonate with us more than others, but we must communicate to all students that we advocate for them and recognize their inherent value.

In our rush to enforce consequences, we sometimes overlook the need to help students understand the impact of their actions. They need to feel that they are still loved and supported, even when they make mistakes. Additionally, educators must be genuine and honest with their students about their missteps.

Our interactions with parents should mirror this openness. Just because we hold a degree in education doesn't mean we have all the answers. Teachers and parents should work in partnership to foster a strong classroom community rather than creating an adversarial dynamic that diminishes parents' roles. Such conflicts can lead to a challenging year devoid of essential support.

I've found that classrooms function best when both parents and students feel valued and happy. That said, there will always be difficult parents who are hard to please, no matter how much effort you invest. These situations can be discouraging and may lead us to question our purpose. Still, we must remember that our goal is to make a difference—sometimes simply by changing a single student's perception of themselves.

Reflections

As an educator, you can empower parents and your colleagues to strive to impact the lives of the families we come across daily. Honestly, I have been discouraged by my colleagues more than my parents. I have had to remind myself of my purpose. My purpose is to serve others; even when they come against you, you can not forget your why. It is not to be teacher of the year on paper. It is to be the teacher of the year in the hearts of the students, parents, and other individuals you may contact daily. Be willing to think outside of self and think about the needs of others.

PRACTICAL TIPS FOR EDUCATORS

1. Trust + Compassion + Unity + Building Relationships
Trust + Compassion + Unity + Building Relationships = Team
Teams built on trust empower relationships between students and staff.

2. Students and Parents are Essential
Students and parents are essential to the team. Parents are vital partners in their children's education, working alongside teachers to support learning and growth inside and outside the classroom.

3. Collaboration Between All
Collaboration between all educators is vital for the success of students and teachers. Educators must collaborate with their colleagues and students to support their social and academic development.

4. Advocate for Student Needs
Advocate for students and their needs; sometimes, this means standing alone. Advocating for students requires unwavering commitment, and sometimes, this means standing alone to ensure their voices and best interests are prioritized.

5. Empower Students to Advocate
Encourage and empower students to advocate for themselves. Students should be encouraged to advocate for themselves, while educators must advocate on their behalf and foster their ability to do so independently.

CULTIVATING KNOWLEDGE AND WONDER

ABOUT LaKEETA Q. PRUNTY

LaKeeta Q. Prunty has been a dedicated advocate for families and students in her community for nearly two decades. With a dual degree in Psychology and Marketing Management from Arkansas State University and a Master's in Cross-Categorical Special Education from Grand Canyon University, she brings a well-rounded and compassionate approach to education. Currently pursuing her Doctorate at Abilene Christian University, LaKeeta is deeply passionate about cultivating strong relationships with students, nurturing their self-confidence, and providing the support they need to excel both academically and personally. Her commitment to education is driven by her desire to empower the next generation.

CONNECT WITH LAKEETA Q. PRUNTY

in @LakeetaPrunty
@cvnresolutions
@pruntyinprogress06

LAKEETA Q. PRUNTY

PART 3
TRANSFORM

" Just as a compass points the way toward new horizons, transformation charts a path of meaningful change that impacts individuals and the world around them. It is the ultimate goal of leadership and education - creating lasting change that extends beyond the moment, reshaping individuals, institutions, and communities.

– Cicely Kelly Ward

CULTIVATING KNOWLEDGE AND WONDER

TAISHA CLAYTOR STEELE

"In every decision, I choose to lead with love and justice, believing that only when we lift each other can we truly rise."

- Taisha Claytor Steele

Chapter 8

Leading with Love, Light, and Justice

by: Taisha Claytor Steele

The first time I grasped the power of leadership, I found myself in a busy hallway. Students hurried past me while teachers scrambled to prepare for the day ahead. The air was thick with the unmistakable energy of a typical morning—chaos, excitement, anxiety, and hope. In that moment, I realized my role as a school counselor extended far beyond advocating for students; I also needed to champion the educators around me—exhausted, overworked, and often overlooked.

This realization dawned on me: leadership couldn't be confined to the four walls of my counseling office. My purpose expanded into a broader mission: to lead with love, light, and justice for students and educators. Leadership isn't about authority or control. It's about empowering others to reach their fullest potential and creating spaces where everyone can thrive.

My journey began as a school counselor, where I spent a decade listening to the heart-wrenching stories of children burdened by challenges too heavy for their young shoulders. Those one-on-one conversations revealed the true essence of advocacy. My understanding deepened when I stepped into the role of counseling coordinator at a Title I school while pursuing my administrative leadership degree. I became acutely aware of the profound inequities affecting children and educators nationwide.

In that role, the education landscape unfolded before me: underfunded classrooms, overwhelmed educators, and policies that often felt disconnected from the very people they were meant to support. Advocacy has always been a core part of my work. Still, this experience illuminated a crucial truth: the adults in our educational systems—teachers, counselors, and administrators—also needed a fierce advocate. My purpose crystallized to ensure educators had the relationships, growth opportunities, psychological safety, and working conditions necessary to give their best every day.

Navigating the complexities of leadership, I recognized that my influence extended to systems, policies, and cultures, impacting everyone. Being an advocate wasn't merely about raising my voice in need; it required intentionality, empathy, and a fierce commitment to doing what was right. This realization drove me to lead with love, light, and justice, fueled by the belief that every individual in our schools—students and educators alike—deserves respect, dignity, and the chance to thrive. Each of these elements is vital, but together, they form the foundation of a transformative leadership style that fosters growth, equity, and lasting impact.

Leading with Love

How can leading with love transform how we support and empower others, particularly in moments of crisis and uncertainty?

At the heart of effective leadership is a profound commitment to the well-being and growth of others. Leading with love fosters a nurturing environment where individuals feel seen, valued, and empowered. It requires patience, empathy, and a deep understanding of human experience.

In my leadership journey, I have witnessed how love can be transformative. As a leader, I've always approached my work with a commitment to care for those I serve. I have always attempted to understand their challenges and aspirations, whether it's students, educators, school administrators, or staff. Leading with love means recognizing that every person has a unique story, including struggles and strengths.

As a district-level leader during the COVID-19 pandemic, I encountered many dedicated educators facing unprecedented challenges. One standout was Mia, an elementary school counselor overwhelmed by the demands of remote learning while juggling her family's health concerns. When she reached out, feeling lost and inadequate, it became a critical moment for both of us—an opportunity to lead with love.

I created a safe space for Mia to express her frustrations. Validating her feelings showed her that she was not alone in her struggles. Active listening is a powerful tool in leadership, reminding educators that their voices matter. Together, we devised practical strategies to alleviate her stress. This joint planning process empowered Mia and reinforced her sense of control over her situation. I made it a priority to regularly check in with Mia, emphasizing the importance of self-care and reassuring her that it was acceptable to take breaks. By genuinely caring for her well-being, I aimed to cultivate a culture of mutual support and connection.

Recognizing that many educators were struggling, I worked with my team to initiate virtual wellness workshops focusing on mental health and self-care. These sessions fostered community and allowed educators to share their vulnerabilities, reinforcing that seeking help is okay.

Leading with love during the pandemic was about more than addressing immediate needs; it was about nurturing a supportive community where educators like Mia could thrive despite the chaos.

This experience reaffirmed my belief that compassion is the cornerstone of effective leadership, particularly in times of crisis. It also reminded me that leadership grounded in love isn't just about the actions of one individual; it's about cultivating a supportive community where everyone can thrive.

Leading with Light

How can leaders bring light to moments of confusion, offering guidance that sparks clarity and ignites collective purpose?

While love is the foundation, light is what guides. Leading with light means illuminating the way forward and offering hope, clarity, and direction when the path ahead seems uncertain. It's about helping others see beyond the immediate challenges and envision what's possible. Light brings focus, perspective, and optimism, especially in times of darkness or difficulty.

Sometimes, leading with light means mediating conflicts among colleagues to foster collaboration. In one instance, two colleagues clashed over their desired solution to a problem, creating tension that impacted team morale.

Recognizing the potential impact on crucial programs, I stepped in to facilitate a conversation in a safe space where my colleagues could share their perspectives openly. As they listened to one another, defensiveness gradually gave way to understanding. My role was to guide the discussion toward finding common ground, emphasizing their shared goal of solving the problem.

Together, we identified strategies that incorporated elements from both approaches, transforming their conflict into an opportunity for growth. This process allowed diverse ideas to flourish, benefiting and strengthening our team's culture.

By leading with light in such situations, I learned that leadership involves illuminating the possibilities that arise from conflict and helping others unite toward a shared vision. This approach enhances collaboration and fosters an environment where everyone feels empowered to contribute.

In education, leading with light often means illuminating new ways of thinking and doing. It's about being a visionary and encouraging innovation through new teaching methods, technology, or community partnerships. It's not enough to simply manage. We must inspire, uplift, and light the way toward a better future for everyone involved.

Leading with Justice

How can leaders ensure their actions actively dismantle barriers and create equitable opportunities for all, especially those who have been historically marginalized?

If love is the heart and light is the vision, justice is the action. Leading with justice means fighting for equity and righting wrongs. It's about ensuring that everyone—regardless of race, gender, socioeconomic status, or background—can succeed and thrive.

For me, leading with justice has always been non-negotiable. In every leadership role, advocating for racial and social justice has been at the forefront of my work. Leadership is about serving those in front of you and dismantling the barriers preventing others from getting to the table.

In one position, as a leader, I recognized the systemic bias that had historically contributed to the underrepresentation of marginalized racial groups in leadership positions within our company. To address this injustice, I initiated work with colleagues to implement initiatives to promote diversity, inclusion, and justice.

One crucial step was to provide bias awareness training to all hiring managers and recruiters. This training helped individuals identify and challenge their unconscious biases, which could inadvertently impact the hiring process. By becoming more aware of their biases, hiring managers and recruiters could make more equitable hiring decisions.

We implemented measures to disseminate our job postings widely to ensure we reached a diverse pool of candidates. This included partnering with organizations that promoted diversity in the workplace, which could help us connect with qualified candidates from underrepresented groups.

Furthermore, we adopted a structured interview process that focused on skills, experience, and qualifications rather than subjective factors that could perpetuate bias. This ensured that all candidates were evaluated on a level playing field.

To provide opportunities for growth and development, we established mentorship programs that paired experienced leaders with promising employees from underrepresented groups. These mentorships offered guidance, support, and valuable insights on career advancement.

Finally, we implemented transparent promotion processes based on objective criteria and communicated clearly to all employees. This helped ensure that promotions were fair and equitable and that all employees clearly understood the expectations and requirements for advancement.

By taking these steps, we were actively working to create

a more equitable and inclusive workplace where individuals from all backgrounds had equal opportunities to succeed.

Justice also means advocating for systemic change. It requires us to speak truth to power, to challenge policies and practices that perpetuate injustices, and to push for reforms that create a more just and equitable society. In my current role, this means working with legislators, school boards, and community activists to advocate for equitable funding for schools, fair wages for educators, and policies that support the holistic development of all students.

Leading with justice takes work. It often means going against the status quo, facing resistance, and making difficult decisions. But it is essential. Without justice, leadership becomes hollow—devoid of the deeper purpose that drives real, lasting change.

Moments of Reflection

How can leading with love, light, and justice influence the relationships and dynamics within your educational community?

Reflecting on my journey as a leader, I realize that love, light, and justice are not isolated concepts but interwoven principles guiding every action and decision. Each complements the other, creating a holistic approach to leadership that empowers, uplifts and drives real, meaningful change.

Leading with love is a powerful reminder that leadership is fundamentally about people. It's about recognizing the full humanity of others, providing support, and fostering an environment where they feel valued and empowered. Love is the cornerstone of trust and growth, nurturing individuals and communities in ways that promote their well-being.

Leading with light is about vision. It involves shedding light on possibilities when the path seems uncertain and guiding others toward a shared purpose. As leaders, we are called to illuminate new ways of thinking, inspire innovation, and help others see beyond their current struggles toward a brighter future.

But **leading with justice** is where love and light take action. Justice is the work of dismantling inequities, advocating for those whose voices are silenced, and ensuring that everyone—regardless of their identity and background—has access to the opportunities they deserve. Justice ensures that the love we show and the light we provide lead to tangible, equitable outcomes.

As I continue to lead, these three principles are central to my practice. They are not simply ideals but imperatives that guide my actions. Together, they challenge me to be intentional, compassionate, and bold in creating spaces where everyone—students, educators, and communities—can thrive.

Leadership grounded in love, light, and justice is not just about personal success. It becomes a catalyst for collective empowerment and systemic transformation. It challenges us not only to lead for today but also to build a more inclusive and just tomorrow for all.

To cultivate effective leadership, it is essential to foster a heightened awareness of one's thoughts and feelings, which enables thoughtful interactions and clear responses to others. Understanding the impact of our presence and treating feedback as a valuable opportunity for growth can enhance personal and collective development. Nurturing authentic relationships through active engagement demonstrates a commitment to truly understanding and supporting others.

Leading with empathy emphasizes the importance of prioritizing individuals' well-being over mere outcomes while encouraging diverse perspectives in discussions. It fosters an inclusive environment where everyone feels respected and valued. Additionally, by supporting individual strengths through mentorship and guidance, leaders empower others to realize their potential and celebrate their unique contributions.

PRACTICAL TIPS FOR EDUCATORS

1. Self-Awareness
Practice self-awareness, which helps you respond to people without personal emotions clouding your judgment. Another aspect of self-awareness is understanding how people experience you. Always provide opportunities for feedback and view it as a gift.

2. Connections and Relationships
Build genuine connections and relationships where you practice active listening.

3. Lead with the Heart
Lead with the heart, not just the mind. Demonstrate that you care for people as humans, not just outputs.

4. Inclusivity
Include diverse voices at the decision-making table to foster an inclusive work environment where everyone feels like they belong.

5. Coaching and Mentoring
Develop individual talents through coaching and mentoring. This allows you to acknowledge people's greatness and help them find their strengths.

ABOUT TAISHA CLAYTOR STEELE

Taisha Claytor Steele is a visionary leader dedicated to advancing justice and equity through compassionate leadership. Grounded in the belief that authentic leadership is about serving others, Taisha strives to create spaces where people feel seen, heard, and empowered to contribute their unique gifts. Leading with a deep sense of purpose, Taisha champions collaboration, diversity, and the power of collective action. With a focus on love and justice, Taisha is committed to shaping leaders driven by empathy and the desire to build a more equitable and inclusive future for all.

CONNECT WITH TAISHA CLAYTOR STEELE

- taisha-steele-eds
- @taisha_inspires
- @taisha_inspires

CULTIVATING KNOWLEDGE AND WONDER

MACHELLE BROWN

"To be a true leader, you have to be willing to face ugly truths so that you can change the trajectory and forge a positive path where we all continue to learn from our mistakes and become better people."

- *Machelle Brown*

Chapter 9

Building A Climate Of Trust

by: Machelle Brown

Teachers are challenged to wear many hats they did not choose, and the demands from outside influencers are overwhelming. Students are plagued with challenges of self-awareness and self-acceptance as they try to fit into a mold constricted by measurements they can't bend. The result can be devastating when these challenges collide in an already volatile environment. This is never good, especially when it involves a student and a teacher.

The Story of Chris

I knew my day was quickly altered when I heard the uncontrollable, inconsolable screams of anger coming from one of my students as he was guided to the office. His clenched fists and heavy breathing told me something terrible had happened.

It was close to the end of the school day when I heard the piercing sound of anger coming down the 400 hall. A female teacher, Ms. Carey, escorted a male student to the AP office. He was yelling and screaming, quite upset.

I am very familiar with this student. His name is Chris.

I have never seen Chris this angry. I asked the teacher what happened, and she said she did not know. She says, " I just heard all the ruckus, and I stepped out and brought him down to the office."

Chris interjects, "I'm going to beat that bitch ass!" Who? I ask. He screams, "Ms. Robinson!"

I look toward the teacher, and she shrugs her shoulders. I tell the teacher that she can return to her class. I have questions for her, but they will have to wait.

I get Chris to calm down, and he says, "You can ask Coach Peterson. He was there. He saw what she tried to do to me."

I am now wondering why the female teacher brought the student to the office, not the male coach. Chris recounts that Ms. Robinson started talking crazy to him in class and disrespecting him. So he got disrespectful to her and started to walk out of class. She began to follow him toward the door, and when he turned back to get his backpack, she pushed against him. He pushed back and turned again toward the door to leave. He says she shoved him out the door, and he kicked his leg toward her before the door could close. Ms. Robinson jerked the door wider and started coming at him.

"She better be glad Coach Peterson came!" Chris gruffly mumbles under his breath.

I am thinking in my head, what in the world just happened in that classroom? I took Chris to an empty office to give him a cool down and let him write down what he had just told me. I called Coach Peterson's room to tell him I needed a statement. The phone line is busy. It is still busy when I wait a few minutes and try again. I decided to walk to the hallway to give statement forms to all three teachers.

When I passed Ms. Carey's class, I saw that she was on her class phone, which is more than likely why I could *not get a free line. I decided to give her the statement form on my way back. I continued down the hallway, and as I reached Ms. Robinson's room, I noticed that she, too, was on her class phone. I know that she and Ms. Carey are talking to each other. I can imagine what the conversation is about.*

As I open Ms. Robinson's door, she quickly hangs up the phone and approaches me. She looks so flustered. I ask her if she needs to step out. She says she will be fine since the class is almost over and she has the last period off. I tell her I need a written statement. She takes a deep breath and shakes her head from side to side. She looks depleted. Whatever happened has taken a toll on her. I try to reassure her that everything will be ok. I don't think she hears me. She told me she would write it as soon as the period was over and bring it to my office.

I continue to coach Peterson and Ms. Carey's classes to let them know I need written statements. They both indicate they don't know what happened but will write what they heard.

Back in my office, I called Chris' mom to let her know that I was investigating an incident that happened. She asked me if she needed to leave work, and I told her no since it was the end of the day. We scheduled a meeting for the next morning.

I check the cameras to see if I can gather any additional information. When they are working and at just the right angle, the cameras can provide a lot of clarifying information when others become "forgetful" in the heat of the moment or do not "see" what really happened amid all the mayhem. Even with the cameras, I am cautious because they do not tell me the mitigating circumstances that may have preceded what is on camera.

What I now see is very disturbing. I take a look from a

CULTIVATING KNOWLEDGE AND WONDER

different camera view. I backtracked and followed Chris from the beginning of the transition to the class. Nothing was out of the norm. I fast-forward to the other two teachers becoming involved in the chaos spilling out of the class. I see what appears to be a sense of urgency as they rush to the aid of···The teacher? The student? I am not sure.

The cameras pick up no sound. I am just watching this silent movie unfold before me.

I can't see what happened in the classroom before the hallway spillage, but I can tell that things must have gotten very intense from what is picked up on camera when the door flies open.

As the class period is about to end, I save the video footage and go to the hallway for duty. A student from Ms. Robinson's class quickly rushes to me and whispers, "Candace has the video," before she hurries.

After the transition, I called Candace to my office. I am not surprised that Candace had the wherewithal to record the incident on her phone. I am sure she is not the only one who recorded the incident, but since I am told she did, I want to see what I know is about to be passed around if it has not already.

When Candace enters my office, she immediately says, "I know why you called me here. It is because of what happened with Chris and Ms. Robinson, right?" I asked her to tell me what happened. She says, "I have the video. At least some of it." She then pauses, realizing she just admitted to having her phone out in class, which she knows is against the rules. "You not gon' take my phone, are you?" I assure her that I will not take her phone this time. She takes the phone out of her purse and punches in her password. When she pulled the video up, she handed me her phone. I can now see what happened inside the *class, at least when she started recording. Her footage is in full technicolor with vibrantly clear sound.*

From the angle of Candace's video, she was seated in the back corner of the room. She was able to capture the span of the whole classroom. I see a class full of students who are eyewitnesses to the chaos that has ensued and disrupted their learning. I can only imagine what they will tell their parents when they get home. For some, this is hilarious entertainment, and they want to see more. They are seen jumping up and down, beating on their desks to incite more chaos. For others, this is a moment of fear, shock, and disbelief. You see them sit stunned in their seats while those close to the action race to the back of the class to get away from it all.

This is a lot to take in. My heart breaks for everyone in that classroom, especially Chris and Ms. Robinson.

When I have to conduct an investigation like this, I do not always divulge what I see on camera. Not at first. When I show camera footage to those involved, I am careful not to give my perspective or opinion of what I see and how I see it. I want the individuals to be able to provide their own perspectives and opinions. This shows me the lens from which their thought processes are based. It tells me if they are looking at it objectively or subjectively. It also helps me to look at the footage again from different viewpoints. It allows me to hear from them what can't be heard on camera. It provides me with the antecedent events that led up to what I see on camera. I can then gather all these missing pieces to the puzzle and try to put them together. This helps me respond to each individual involved based on their perspective, with all the feelings and emotions that come with what has just transpired in the heat of the moment.

In this case, I have to ensure the safety of both my students and my teacher. How I respond will be pivotal to both of them and their ability to trust my judgment and know that I have their well-being at heart. I have to think about Chris' mother and the other staff members, including Ms. Carey and Coach Peterson, who are now watching how I move forward. Will they be able to trust me after my investigation is concluded? Will I have a student who feels no one ever takes his side or believes him? Who thinks that "principals always believe what the teacher says?" Will I have a teacher who feels that, once again, students "get away with everything and administration never supports the teacher?"

I have to ensure that everyone is heard, seen, and supported. Above all, I must help right all the wrongs that brought us to this situation.

REFLECTION

As an administrator, I do not have all the answers. However, I know that whatever decision I make will affect several stakeholders. My stakeholders include the single mother raising boys, like Chris, the grandmother who is a feisty, former track star in her glory days who has had to "turn off my pot of greens" to come to the school to lend her support; The father whose first encounter with me was angrily shouting, "Y'all know he can't read" before we, together, built a school and home tutorial plan to support and strengthen his reading skills. My stakeholder is the Hispanic mom who angrily points at me and says we are "racistas" until she realizes I am the one who spoke to her in Spanish over the phone.

My stakeholders are first-year teachers who want to make a difference even on tough days and veteran teachers who have "seen and heard it all" and still choose to show up every day for our students. They are watching me each day. They are entrusting me with both their professional and, at times, personal fears, celebrations, and challenges. I must lead by example.

My stakeholders are my students, too. From the one who hides the self-inflicted scars, the one trying to manage the bottled-up emotions from pain, anger, and uncertainty, to the "popular kid" trying to keep up an image, even when it is difficult, and even those who are nonverbal. I must speak up for them all and continue to build and maintain their trust.

I never want to base my decisions on what is "politically correct." This makes things difficult only because it sometimes means a backlash from those who prefer I use politically correct standards. Those standards make decisions easy because they protect and shield us from facing ugly truths. I believe that to be a true leader, you have to be willing to face ugly truths. You have to face them before you can change the trajectory and forge a positive path where we all continue to learn from our mistakes and become better people, educators, and mentors to those we serve.

PRACTICAL TIPS FOR EDUCATORS

1. Put yourself, your family, and your health first.
2. Do your best and do what is best for your students. You are the one who more than likely knows them better than any administrator or district leader.
3. Know your data, but most importantly, know the students behind those data. Let that be your guide to what you and your students need.
4. Lead with grace and mercy for students and staff. Everyone has a story, and sometimes you may be the antagonist in someone else's. That is ok. Perspectives are valued but can be challenged by another's viewpoint.
5. Remember that every day is a new day to reflect, learn, and grow.

CONNECT WITH MACHELLE BROWN

• • • • • • • • • • • • •

in Machelle Brown
◉ @Machelle.Brown.9
X @MachelleDBrown

ABOUT MACHELLE BROWN

Machelle Brown is the author of Authentically Me: Flaws & All – From Teacher to A.P., a powerful memoir that captures her transformative journey through the educational system. With candid reflections on the trials and triumphs of her early career, Brown's story is an inspiring testament to resilience, growth, and leadership in education. Her second book, Gabriel: The Silent Truth, offers a gripping investigative account of a non-verbal special needs student's mysterious injury at school, shining a spotlight on the critical need for advocacy, accountability, and justice within the education system.

Beyond her own writing, Machelle is dedicated to nurturing the voices of young writers through her "Lemon Cookie Project," an initiative that helps first-time student authors bring their stories to life. Notable works from this program include The Draconic Evolution by Xavier Guillory and The Strength of a Mother and Daughter by Hawa Aline and Alice Juma, which reflect her commitment to empowering students to find their voice and share their unique perspectives with the world.

Machelle Brown's work transcends the classroom and the page, sparking important conversations about equity, leadership, and the transformative power of storytelling. Through her writing and mentorship, she advocates for a more inclusive, just, and student-centered education system that uplifts all voices, especially those that are often unheard.

CULTIVATING KNOWLEDGE AND WONDER

DEITRA COLQUITT

"Leadership is a beautiful, chaotic journey that pushes people beyond what they think is imaginable. Along the way, it is easy to look at someone else's version of leadership and compare yourself to them. There is no comparison. While the road may look the same, it is different."

- *Deitra Colquitt*

Chapter 10

Not Good, Better, or Best: Just Different

by: Deitra Colquitt

I am a staunch believer in shared understanding, which means everyone is on the same page about what things mean. Therefore, beginning my story with definitions from the Merriam-Webster Dictionary is only fitting. While these words may be elementary, life's experiences often shape and mold their meanings beyond their dictionary definitions. Let's get started!

Term	Definition
Good	adequate, satisfactory
Better	comparative of good; more advantageous or effective
Best	superlative of good; most productive of good: offering or producing the greatest advantage, utility, or satisfaction
Different	partly or totally unlike in nature, form, or quality; dissimilar

I want to begin by saying that this story applies to anyone who has occupied a role at some point in their life and career. I have stepped into several roles: wife, mother, teacher, instructional coach, and principal. Aside from being a mother and wife, serving as a school principal has been one of my most challenging roles. The principalship has pushed me to maintain a constant state of reflection and truly see myself—flaws and all. My ability to reflect has manifested in various forms: comparison to others (*Not good*), arguments with my husband (*Yikes!*), the Calm app (*Yass!!!*), and inconsistent journaling (*I'm human*).

And as you know, comparisons with others have brought us together. It is so easy to be on the outside looking in and make inferences that are not grounded in reality. I have learned that the best and most challenging mode of reflection for me is stillness. When I have taken the time to sit with myself, let my guard down, and be in the moment, I am able to be balanced and more introspective. In times of stillness, I can see both the present and past while navigating the future.

At the start of my tenure, my school district shifted toward a more human-centered approach. I needed to embed empathy, emotional intelligence, and adaptability into how I showed up as a leader. I believe this approach became especially important given the significant events from 2019 to the present, including the impact of COVID-19, the tragic loss of Black lives at the hands of police and "well-meaning" white people, and the increase in school shootings. Education was evolving to be more customer service-driven. My customers—parents, students, and staff—needed a leader who understood the 'head and heart' of the work. While 'head and heart' work usually refers to Bloom's and Maslow's theories, I believe it extends beyond students and the classroom. For the purpose of this chapter, 'head work' will refer to technical skills, while 'heart work' will refer to people skills. Since life respects no one, all my customers required compassion and care, coupled with clear expectations, to ensure they thrived and flourished.

In my reality, the world was engulfed in a perpetual state of chaos and confusion, a backdrop that shaped the significance of my story.

> "COVID-19 has brought with it a rise in anti-Asian racism, discrimination, xenophobia, and violence. Students of Asian descent have been experiencing increased bullying in schools and public transportation riders have been violently attacked. Unfortunately, this racism is not new: historically, global crises have led to scapegoating and blaming people of color. School and organizational leaders have an important opportunity to educate students and employees and prevent racist and discriminatory behavior (Alive and Well Communities, nd)."

You might be curious about why this context is crucial to my narrative. Well, I'll tell you! Context is everything, and sometimes, looking in from the outside makes it easy to fall into the comparison trap. Leadership is dynamic, and the skills needed to be successful are not static. What I was navigating as a new leader was markedly different from what my predecessor experienced. COVID-19 shut schools down for months, thrusting educators into a new norm of virtual instruction while claiming many lives. A few years before the pandemic, Ferguson, Missouri, was at the center of national debates and protests following the killing of Michael Brown. For those unfamiliar with Missouri, Ferguson is a municipality within St. Louis, where I reside. My school district, also located in St. Louis, is about 15 minutes away from the site of Michael Brown's tragic death.

To understand the events surrounding the killing of Michael Brown, we must consider the societal tensions that contributed to the unrest. Carol Anderson highlights this perspective, asserting, "When we look back on what happened in Ferguson, Missouri, during the summer of 2014, it will be easy to think of it as yet one more episode of Black rage ignited by yet another police killing of an unarmed African American male. But that has it precisely backward. What we've seen is the latest outbreak of white rage. Sure, it is cloaked in the niceties of law and order, but it is rage nonetheless" (Anderson, 2014). In addition to COVID-19 and racism, there was also an increase in school shootings.

> *"There were more school shootings in 2022 – 46 – than in any year since Columbine. This mirrored America's broader rise in gun violence as it emerged from the pandemic." (U.S. Department of Education, U.S. Secret Service, & Federal Bureau of Investigation, 2019)"*

As you can see, the demands of leadership have extended far beyond academics and school management from 2019 to the present. Some of the harshest realities in the world began colliding simultaneously: food insecurity, implicit biases, death, white saviorism, low expectations, entitlement, mental and physical illnesses, and loneliness, to name just a few. It often felt like I was an octopus in a three-ring circus, juggling twenty balls at once. How's that for imagery?

I faced what felt like unprecedented challenges as a school leader. My new reality required a different approach to serving my school community. There was no clear separation between what was happening in the world and within the school; everything intermingled. My daily focus revolved around establishing a sense of normalcy during these trying times, ensuring that students and teachers were treated with care and concern, and developing plans to address the academic impact of school closures on those most affected by systems that seemed designed for their failure. I did not take my responsibilities lightly.

Every decision mattered, knowing that my actions would ripple through the lives of those I served. I dedicated myself to fostering open lines of communication, recognizing that every voice was vital in our shared journey. As we navigated these turbulent times, I aimed to create a culture of empathy and support. To ensure all stakeholders felt seen and heard, I initiated several opportunities, including:

- **Principal Listening Sessions:** Parents are invited to participate in in-person or virtual meetings without a set agenda, allowing attendees to speak freely with the school leader about their hopes, dreams, and concerns.

- **Community Listening Sessions:** Community stakeholders engage in open forums where specific questions focus on strengthening partnerships between the school and the community.

- **Parent Cafés:** These learning sessions center on specific topics designed to eliminate barriers that families face in participating in their child's education.

- **Student Interviews and Focus Groups:** Conducting one-on-one and small group conversations, these sessions gather insights on topics ranging from student well-being and joy to staff-student interactions.

- **Parent Interviews and Focus Groups:** Similar to student focus groups, these sessions involve one-on-one and small group conversations with parents to discuss their experiences related to well-being and joy, as well as staff-parent interactions.

- **Start, Stop, Continue Reflection with Staff:** This initiative invites staff members to reflect on practices by identifying what should be started, stopped, or continued to enhance the school.

CULTIVATING KNOWLEDGE AND WONDER

Based on the information gathered, I established focused, bite-sized goals to address issues that would strengthen our school community academically, socially, and emotionally.

It would be easy to say that I uplifted my community and that academic performance soared during my tenure, but the reality is far more nuanced. My success didn't come from surpassing my predecessors but from adapting to the unique circumstances I encountered. While it was tempting to view improved suspension rates as a standalone achievement, these changes were a result of implementing progressive discipline and restorative practices rather than any singular triumph of my leadership. Likewise, celebrating the appearance of academic growth on our state assessment might have overlooked the deeper story.

With the adoption of a new rating scale that highlighted growth metrics, my students did meet their growth targets. Without context, it could have been tempting to judge this as a straightforward progression of good, better, and best. However, the dynamics of my situation were different, and it's essential to understand the distinct drivers that shaped this reality.

Various contexts and factors influenced the challenges I faced and my approach to navigating this beautifully complex experience. I quickly learned that success isn't measured solely by numbers or comparisons to past performances; rather, it's deeply rooted in unique circumstances. Each decision was informed by the collective needs and voices of students and staff, reminding me that my journey was not about competition but about growth. As Zen Shin beautifully states, "A flower does not think of competing with the flower next to it. It just blooms."

PRACTICAL TIPS FOR EDUCATORS

1. Identify key drivers that will impact daily decisions and interactions.
2. Set clear goals for your leadership legacy.
3. Learn, grasp, and embrace HUMILITY.
4. Mistakes will happen. Don't waddle in them.
5. Learn to filter through the noise (inside of your head and the chatter of others).

ABOUT DEITRA COLQUITT

Deitra Colquitt is a passionate and dedicated elementary school principal, committed to showcasing the brilliance and potential within the students and community she proudly serves. As a product of the same district where she now leads, Deitra brings a deeply personal connection and a transformative vision, aiming to redefine the narrative for the children in her care. She strives to uplift and empower people of color, fostering an environment where they can thrive in their unique gifts and talents. Deitra is an advocate for educational excellence, a devoted wife to Derrick, and a loving mother to Khloe, Demi, and Trey, balancing her professional life with her dedication to family.

CONNECT WITH DEITRA COLQUITT

in DeitraColquitt

DEITRA COLQUITT

CULTIVATING KNOWLEDGE AND WONDER

REFERENCES

Alive and Well Communities. (n.d.). *Trauma-sensitive practices in the age of COVID-19*. Alive and Well Communities. Retrieved October 1, 2024, from https://www.awcommunities.org/traumasensitivecovid19

American Psychological Association. (2020). *Publication manual of the American Psychological Association* (7th ed.). American Psychological Association.

Anderson, C. (2014, August 29). Ferguson wasn't Black rage against cops. It was white rage against progress. *The Washington Post*. https://www.washingtonpost.com/opinions/ferguson-wasnt-black-rage-against-copsit-was-white-rage-against-progress/2014/08/29/3055e3f4-2d75-11e4-bb9b-997ae96fad33_story.html

Kennedy, E. M. (1968, June 8). Eulogy for Robert F. Kennedy. St. Patrick's Cathedral, New York, NY.

Merriam-Webster. (n.d.-a). *Better*. In *Merriam-Webster.com dictionary*. Retrieved July 28, 2024, from https://www.merriam-webster.com/dictionary/better

Merriam-Webster. (n.d.-b). *Best*. In *Merriam-Webster.com dictionary*. Retrieved July 28, 2024, from https://www.merriam-webster.com/dictionary/best

Merriam-Webster. (n.d.-c). *Different*. In *Merriam-Webster.com dictionary*. Retrieved July 28, 2024, from https://www.merriam-webster.com/dictionary/different

Merriam-Webster. (n.d.-d). *Good*. In *Merriam-Webster.com dictionary*. Retrieved July 28, 2024, from https://www.merriam-webster.com/dictionary/good

Merriam-Webster. (n.d.-e). *Nurture*. In *Merriam-Webster.com dictionary*. Retrieved July 28, 2024, from https://www.merriam-webster.com/dictionary/nurture

OpenAI. (2024). ChatGPT [Large language model]. https://chat.openai.com/chat

U.S. Department of Education, U.S. Secret Service, & Federal Bureau of Investigation. (2019). *Protecting America's schools: A U.S. Secret Service analysis of targeted school violence*. https://www.ed.gov/sites/ed/files/admins/lead/safety/preventingattacksreport.pdf

CULTIVATING KNOWLEDGE AND WONDER

VISIONARY AUTHOR

" This book is more than just a collection of pages. It's a tool for self-reflection and growth, the pedagogical equivalent of a strong cup of coffee—the kind with an extra shot of inspiration—to jumpstart and elevate your teaching and leadership."

- Cicely Kelly Ward

ABOUT CICELY KELLY WARD

Cicely Kelly Ward is an accomplished education professional with over 24 years of experience in the field, including numerous leadership roles. Her expertise is in designing and implementing impactful professional development programs, with a focus on data analysis, professional learning communities, curriculum and instruction, and mentoring. Cicely's diverse background includes district-level management, school administration, and instructional coaching, enabling her to make significant contributions to the ongoing improvement of educational practices and student outcomes. She is also the CEO and lead consultant at Cultivating Knowledge and Wonder, LLC, where she empowers both educators and organizations to enhance teaching, learning, and organizational effectiveness through consulting, professional development, and speaking engagements.

Cicely earned a Bachelor of Science from Alcorn State University and a Master of Education in Administration from Sam Houston State University. She is currently a doctoral candidate in the Organizational Leadership program at Abilene Christian University. A proud member of Delta Sigma Theta Sorority, Incorporated, Cicely is dedicated to both her profession and her community. In her personal time, she enjoys traveling with her husband and cherishes moments spent with family and friends.

CONNECT WITH CICELY KELLY WARD

@CicelyKWard

LearnWithCKW.org

www.ingramcontent.com/pod-product-compliance
Lightning Source LLC
Chambersburg PA
CBHW050528170426
43201CB00013B/2127